The Eberle Named Ray

by Jan Eberle

Cadence Jazz Books   Redwood, New York

Printed in the United States of America

Published by:

Cadence Jazz Books
Cadence Building
Redwood, NY 13679 U.S.A.
ph: 315/287-2852   fax 315/287-2860   email: cjb@cadencebuilding.com

ISBN # 1-881993-41-8

Distributed by:

North Country Distributors
Cadence Building
Redwood, NY 13679
U.S.A.
phone: 315/287-2852   fax: 315/287-2860
email: northcountry@cadencebuilding.com

Table of Contents

Preface

The purpose of this book is to uncover and share a piece of wonderful history. In this case, it is that of a man, the mark he left in musical history and his profound effect on millions of fans and perhaps, most importantly, how those things affected his personal life.

As time ticks by, history slips away from us and if we are interested ... if we are truly yearning to learn ... we will turn around, look over our shoulders, and catch it before it disappears forever. This time, I tap your shoulders and ask you to take a look at the life of my father, Ray Eberle.

Ray Eberle entered a part of our history during a magical time. If that sounds like a cliché, you need only ask people who grew up during World War II. I am confident that fighting a lousy war is not magical, however it was the outside influence of the onset of the Big Band Era that attracted people to dream. Those people made the choice to lose themselves in the realm of magic called music.

In our history, there have been many points in time that are unforgettable ... some more than others. And so, it is on this premise that I have written this book and plan to take you on a journey, not only through history, but into the life of a man referred to by Glenn Miller as The Young Man in the Romance Department.

Although Ray is my father, there was quite a lot of research done for this book. Some of it was fun and some of it was painstakingly hard. Dad's friends and fellow musicians were kind and more than willing to help me piece together a life that was, to me, incomplete. In this, I mean that I could not have possibly known who he really was in, say, 1941 for example for the simple fact that I wasn't born then. And, even though I've been a Big Band enthusiast for many years, I still found myself asking questions about Dad's life that I could not answer. Needless to say, if I had not had the good fortune of finding these friends and co-workers, I might not have completed this work. It is to them that I am eternally grateful.

In 1982, the Louis Miller Museum in Hoosick Falls, New York was founded. This historical place, that honors many local people, such as Grandma Moses, also has an entire room dedicated to Ray and Bob Eberle. I was proud to have 'cut the ribbon', so to speak, in this dedication as it is a permanent place in which to feed those hungry for really good history.

In 1995, my father was posthumously inducted into the Music Hall of Fame in Georgia for his dedication to bringing continued excellence to the state of Georgia during the last years of his historical walk.

I invite you to visit the Georgia Music Hall of Fame in Macon, Georgia, the Georgia Music Walk of Fame annex in Atlanta, Georgia, and the Louis Miller Museum in Hoosick Falls, New York. My father would have wanted to share these things with you.

God, grant me the serenity
To accept the things I cannot change
Courage to change the things I can
And wisdom to know the difference.

Thank you, my very good friends
for your experience,
strength and hope.

School-aged Ray in June 1928.

Chapter One

The day my father died was one of the worst days of my life. I realized that I was not only losing a Daddy, but also that the world was losing a great singer and a very important part of music history. Raymond George Eberle was more than he thought he was to a lot of people. Sometimes I believe he always thought of himself as that *yuck* from Hoosick Falls, New York. No, Dad, that's not a cough medicine. That's where you were from. Rather than lingering on his end, I'd prefer to embrace his beginning and all the stuff in between ... his life.

My grandfather, John Alloicious, was a first generation born American from a family of German descent. In fact, our family name was not originally Eberle. It was Abole. The pronunciation and spelling probably got fouled up at Ellis Island, as did many immigrants' names. My grandmother, on the other hand, had different roots. Margaret O'Brien, also first generation to the United States, was Irish. Her mother, Bridget, who came with her daughter to America, passed on her true Irish features. Margaret had a strong build, olive complexion, dark brown eyes and hair the color of a raven's. She was very outgoing and funny. I give her full credit for passing on the Eberle sense of humor, which is mostly just plain corniness. At any rate, my grandmother and grandfather both ended up in the same area of New York State. I am not sure how they both came to settle near Albany, but that is not as important as the turns their lives took.

Grandpa Jack, as the family called him, was a strong singer. He wasn't professional, but he loved singing opera just the same. On occasion he would meet up with piano players and, with their accompaniment, sing for church functions, dances, and pretty much anyone who would hire him for a few bucks. It was money on the side and he enjoyed himself as well. By day, he was a police officer in the town of Mechanicville, New York.

One day, Grandpa Jack was supposed to sing at a small local function, but he fell short on accompaniment. He went frantically around town searching for anyone who played the piano until he came to a small service station. The owner told Jack he knew a quite accomplished piano player, who lived close by. Grandma Margaret played the piano and with a lot of gusto, from what I've been told. She was just what Jack was looking for, but he really didn't know how much until some dates later. It was so simple, but that's really how it all started. Mr. And Mrs. Jack Eberle settled in Mechanicville, New York.

After talking to family members, I've confirmed that there were thirteen original Eberle children, eight of whom survived. During the early years of the twentieth century, medicine was not nearly as advanced as it is today, therefore, children died from diseases such as tuberculosis, scarlet fever, polio and many other infections that they would not likely die from today. Four of the Eberle children died that way, eight survived and the firstborn died tragically.

Baby Jack was in the hands of his father, one afternoon, at home. Grandpa was not on a shift at the police department and was in charge of watching the baby in Grandmother's absence. As baby Jack sat perched in his high chair, he fell victim to a gunshot wound, which killed him instantly. My grandfather was cleaning his weapon in the kitchen when it discharged, wounding his baby son fatally. From what Dad's siblings have told me, there were not many words spoken about the incident among family members for years. I can only imagine the guilt my grandfather lived with until his own death years later.

My father, Raymond George, was born on January 19th, 1919 in Mechanicville, New York. Uncle Bob was a few years older and Uncle Walt, about eighteen months younger. They were all typical boys who hung around, went to school, did chores and got into usual boy trouble. They were good boys, though, despite their father's firm ways.

Peg and Pat came after the boys, which must have been a relief to my grandmother. And then came another son named Alfred: the last child born before the family moved to Hoosick Falls, New York.

Hoosick Falls was just as country-like as Mechanicville, but the train ran through the town, and there were the falls and river. It seemed to make more sense, as their family grew, to relocate here. In addition, my great grandmother, Bridget, had left the family a hotel in Hoosick, which peaked their innate sense of adventure. Jack quit the police force and off they went to the newly named Hoosick Hotel.

Life was very different in the 1920's and 1930's. There were no televisions, no computers and no malls for Saturday shopping. Instead, there were radios, the mercantile stores and Prohibition. The Hoosick Hotel not only housed its patrons, but also offered my grandmother's cooking and Jack's serving beer at the bar. The patrons gathered on the hotel porch to listen to the latest scores of that day's baseball game. Men wore suits and hats; women wore dresses ... all the time ... everywhere. A sign in the front window could be seen from the road and it read, "Roast Beef Sandwiches and Little Neck Clams, fifteen cents." Do you have any idea how much money people were earning per week then? Twenty dollars? Forty dollars? How much did a dress cost? Two dollars? Less? That boggles my mind.

If I hadn't seen all the men gathered on the porch of the hotel listening to the baseball scores with my own eyes, I wouldn't have believed how simple life really was. That glimpse of history was given to me via an old home video. In that video, Daddy was on a neighboring farm ... chasing chickens and catching them! I watched him in those old movies time after time and he looked like he was truly enjoying those simple things. No matter how worldly he looked in his tuxedo and no matter who he happened to be hanging out with on any given day, my father always remained a simple man. He was not a city boy, although his work made it impossible to avoid that life. In time, he learned to love it, but I know he enjoyed quieter living.

Jack Eberle seemed to have many interests. One involved a Spanish gentleman by the name of Paolino Uzcudun. From what I've been told, he was brought to Hoosick Falls to train for the Heavyweight Boxing Championship. Paolino's training camp was located at the Hans Ehlmer estate just outside Hoosick city limits. Family members believe that Jack was somewhat instrumental in bringing Paolino to Hoosick. Men gathered wearing suits, women, dresses, to watch afternoon training of the young Spaniard. Other families afterward joined our family at Mohawk Trail for a picnic. Old movies are precious to me because I didn't know my grandparents.

My grandmother died almost thirty years before I was born. She and my Uncle Al were going down the hill from the hotel to, believe it or not, fetch a pail of water. Without warning, Grandmother collapsed in the grips of a heart attack and died on the hill before help could arrive. In 1931, she was forty-eight years old. Daddy was about twelve, a hard age to lose a parent as if there is ever a good time: a vulnerable age, the age between childhood and adulthood. My father had plenty of brothers and sisters and a father who loved him deeply, but nothing and no one could replace the burning hole inside Dad from the loss of his mother. I believe it was something he never totally recovered from. It wasn't the last time in his life he suffered a loss like it.

Margaret O'Brien Eberle was the matriarch of the family, of that I am sure. Her sense of humor, piano playing and dancing about must have been everyone's anchor: their beacon. For Dad, it was as if a light went out that never shone again.

Jack married a second time to a woman named Rita, who was the only parent figure of Dad's I ever knew. Rita and Jack had two children named Jackie and Gail—the babies.

Around sixteen, my dad's interest changed from chickens and baseball to young ladies and he began to date. Often, his dates involved going to a dance, although I've never known my father to dance a step. Oh, he had rhythm-a-plenty, but dancing just wasn't something Ray Eberle did. But, Lord, was he handsome! His dates probably never realized he didn't dance. My uncles told me that girls stared at him and flirted constantly. And he kept getting better looking with age.

My father was becoming a man and he looked up to his big brother, Bob, who at about nineteen years old, had begun to take his hobby of singing seriously. Bob, Walt and Dad sang barbershop quartet with the local barber for a while and at a few church functions, but nothing really heavy. All the Eberle kids sang at home a lot because Grandmother played the piano so ferociously that it was hard to stay quiet.

One night, Uncle Bob was singing in a talent show of some sort and was heard by two men in show business who were just starting to make a mark in music themselves. These musicians, who happened to be brothers, were forming an orchestra and wanted a singer who not only possessed a unique style, but was also one the ladies could appreciate. Tommy and Jimmy Dorsey liked Uncle Bob's voice so much they hired him that evening! His style was similar to what Grandpa Jack's may have been like as it had an operatic quality to it. Very powerful. My grandfather was very happy and enthused for Bob perhaps because he saw a little bit of what he, himself, had wanted to pursue.

The Dorsey Brothers' band played a music that was different from what Jack had grown up with. As the mid-1930's unfolded there emerged from the shadows of depression a new era. People began sensing an excitement about the music, although few could have guessed its future magnitude and historical value. It was the beginning of the Big Band Era and Uncle Bob was in it from the start. What a ride!

In 1936 and 1937, my father was still in high school and loving the young ladies, but I know he was intrigued just thinking about his big brother singing in front of large, eager crowds every night. He and Uncle Bob always had a pretty good relationship; they were brothers in every sense of the word. Dad looked up to Bob and regarded what he did with the Dorseys as a class act. Basically, he envied him, in a good way and without sibling rivalry. Coming into adulthood himself, my father was anxious to get a real glimpse of the outside world and the big city! Over the years he had talked repeatedly about the decision he almost made to stay in Hoosick Falls. He always said he pictured himself sitting on some beer barrel in the corner, shucking clams like some yuck: his word for country folk. Considering his roots, he meant no harm.

I understand that Dad periodically sang with the Don Weston Band in New England for local functions, but nothing that would've put him on the map considering what was happening in New York City. My uncle began inviting him to the city to watch him perform and shmooze with the ladies. Dad eagerly took him up on it and caught as many trains as necessary to get there.

Then, quite suddenly, The Dorseys split their band due to personal conflicts. It was both a shame and a blessing. They were so good together and no one likes to see brothers have that kind of falling out. The good thing that came from it is that there were now two incredible bands with new singers and songs. Tommy Dorsey was known for being one of the best trombone players in the business, his style and ability admired by many. Brother Jimmy was a fine clarinetist and alto saxman with great arranging ideas. Both brothers were good businessmen and had vision enough for ten men when it came to the new sounds of the Big Band Era. Uncle Bob went with the new Jimmy Dorsey Orchestra, as did his singing companion, Helen O'Connell.

My father was in the final stretch of high school and began to think seriously about his future. He liked what he saw and heard in New York City and it lit a fire inside. He was proud of Bob, and I believe he wanted that life more than he ever admitted. He wanted a piece of the excitement for himself. His mind was made up, but joining Glenn Miller's band shortly after was quite a bit of happenstance.

Helen O'Connell, singer for the Jimmy Dorsey Orchestra, once said, "If I'd known I was in the middle of an era, I would've paid more attention." That may have been true for a lot of musicians during the Big Band explosion because these musicians knew they had not experienced anything that came close to it. It was enormous, but as Helen stated, no one was aware of this history-making time until it was well on its way. Glenn Miller was probably no different.

Glenn Miller formed his second or third band in 1937, mostly for recording tunes, but soon disbanded because he couldn't tolerate the drinking and bar scenes. With Prohibition a distant memory, everyone was drinking, and, drinking a lot. That was the most rampant form of socializing and an example of what happens to the human psyche when deprived of something for long periods of time. Miller supposedly only drank socially, but even so found himself more and more surrounded by it. In 1938 he formed yet another orchestra, and brought with him a hand-picked group of talented musicians. After carefully selecting his instrumental members, Glenn knew he needed a great singer because competition among the bands was already tough.

Billy May, speaks about that time:

> *I knew your Uncle Bob first. I played trumpet and arranged for Charlie Barnet's band. Then I approached Jimmy Dorsey for a job, but that didn't work out. Finally, I joined Glenn's band and swiftly became a "red shirt." A "red shirt" was one of a group that didn't like Glenn. I joined Miller in November of 1940. We were playing at the Pennsylvania Hotel when I first met Ray and I remember Roosevelt was elected for the first term. The hotel was like a ghost town ... everyone was at home glued to their radios! Glenn was really mad!*
>
> *Anyway, I thought Ray was a real good singer. He really didn't hang out with the rest of the guys in the band. It's not that he was conceited, but I guess he was just a loner. Your Dad was a great guy to be with and a real jokester. We got to be pretty good friends especially when we later moved to California. We'd play darts for hours. Ray was a funny, talented man.*
>
> *It is evident to me that Ray was greatly responsible for Glenn Miller's success and was clearly an asset to him. I believe he was hand-picked because he sounded and looked a lot like Bob, who was already popular and well liked by most. From the onset of the big bands, Glenn was very impressed with Bob's style and probably would've liked to have had him for his own band. It's very likely that your father was hired based on his strength that he might've been another Bob. All in all, Glenn couldn't have done any better than he did when he hired Ray.*

There is no doubt in my mind that my father was totally in tune with what was happening in the world of music. He loved the whole scene. He loved going to New York City, to the excitement, the big bands, the fans and he loved going to see his brother sing. It was a kick for him to see Bob as a new celebrity, flirting with the girls and being adored by the fans. I think Dad secretly dreamed of that for himself. He liked singing, loved girls, and knew that the fans adored the big band singers. Bob was handsome and sang sweetly, what's not to like about that? However, Ray was still a country boy at heart and while visiting was one thing, living that life was another.

Most of the bandleaders who were forming bands in the '30's had been starving artists together in other people's bands and knew each other on some level. Many of the upcoming band leaders had played with Paul Whiteman at some time or another. Miller, Goodman, Dorsey, were all from the same stock, so to speak, and waited for the golden opportunity to become well known with their unique styles. Glenn knew Jimmy Dorsey and his manager and arranged to meet them at the Hotel New Yorker one night to watch Bob sing. Glenn admired Uncle Bob's voice as well as his good looks and, given the chance, he'd have chosen Bob for his own band.

Miller was looking for someone as handsome and with a set of pipes to go with the looks. By sheer happenstance, Uncle Bob had invited my Dad to the Hotel New Yorker the same night Glenn was there. Glenn was hoping to talk to Jimmy and Bob to find out if they knew of anyone who could fit his bill. Just as planned, Glenn arrived shortly before the show started and took a seat at Jimmy Dorsey's table.

Moments later, filled with excitement, my father bounded down the center aisle toward the stage to greet his big brother. Glenn saw Ray pass right by his table, and immediately noticed the close family resemblance. Glenn actually did a double take because, at first, he mistook Ray for Bob. My father, oblivious to Glenn's presence and to the striking impression he had made on him, didn't know Miller was searching for a singer. Miller confronted Jimmy and his manager about the strange events and, upon hearing who my father was, became still more intrigued. At the end of the show, Jimmy called Bob over and asked him about my father, and Bob told him that Ray had done some local engagements with a small-time band, but the bottom line was that they'd all have to ask Dad. That was the first time Dad met Glenn, and Glenn, taken by his looks, set up an audition for Dad later that week. Miller clearly hoped that Dad's voice would impress him as much as his good looks had. It turned out that Glenn's

The Eberle Named Ray

expectations were satisfied; my father's voice matched his dreamy looks and he was hired on the spot.

The worst part for Dad was having to go back to Hoosick Falls to break the news to Grandpa Jack. He supported one singer in the family, but he didn't know if he'd do it a second time. My father was still a few months from finishing high school and he was supposed to meet Glenn up in Boston almost immediately for rehearsals and their first engagement. Everything turned out all right with Jack, he wouldn't stop any of his children from following their dreams, even if he did want to be a dumb singer.

ay, Glenn and Paula Kelly — something is funny?

Chapter Two

Life as a band singer was very different for Dad compared to his first nineteen years in upstate New York. Shucking clams quickly became but a memory. He had successfully prepared with Miller's band for their opening at the Raymor Ballroom in Boston in April of 1938. I'm sure my father was anxious, but at the same time exhilarated from the intense energy of the fans. They used to gather close to the stage with droves of girls encircling the singer's platform like a human buffer. How overwhelming it all must have been. Most of the musicians in the band had never been exposed to the volume and intensity of these crowds.

One such musician was a tenor saxophone player and novelty singer named Gordon Beneke. Most called him "Tex." It's been said that some close to Glenn at that time doubted his eagerness to bring people like Tex and my Dad on board. History has proven Miller's instincts in this case to be sound. Tex was one of the finest sax men in the business and he added class, charm and wit to the organization. He was solid and knew his job and was in part responsible for Glenn's success.

Beneke gave one hundred percent and would've given the shirt off his back to just about anyone, and he remained loyal to Miller long after Glenn's disappearance and death. Tex told me it wasn't always easy but, as a young twenty-something year-old kid with stars in his eyes and a tuned instrument, he was ready for action.

Singer Marion Hutton was also on board. Her specialty was the novelty Swing tune. She was a darling and quite a "show woman." She knew her strengths and used them well.

My father, still the kid in the first months, remained persistent in pleasing Miller. He sang tunes in ungodly keys and kept the girls interested with his looks and charms. It was Miller's show. His name was up front. The musicians played his famous, unique sound, heard mainly in the octave split of the sax section, Dad sang his heart out on ballads while Marion and The Modernaires kept the kids dancing. But the glory went to the bandleaders; the singers and musicians were nothing but players. Glenn Miller was a lot of things, but most of his own musicians admitted he wasn't a great trombone player. He was, however, a great businessman and the band covered him with their playing and Dad and Marion covered him with their singing. But it was the bandleader who naturally got the credit. The bandleaders had what most of these kids (the musicians) lacked: longevity in show business, lots of money and financial backing and the ability to push hard in a business the kids scarcely knew. But what an education. My father began with Miller's outfit making something like thirty-five dollars a week: not bad compared to shucking clams.

Shortly after they began performing together, the Glenn Miller band of 1938 took off with its great group of singers, instrumentalists and arrangers, fresh and eager to show off Miller's new sound. It was genius and, like most genius, fundamentally simple. The placement for his sax section was the main reason for his unique sound. Miller knew what he had in his band and in his sound. He was a shrewd businessman and surrounded himself with a close and loyal staff. Boarding this train, my father had no idea what he was getting into; it was a locomotive that pulled out quickly and he never looked back and it never slowed down. Once their popularity took off, it was out of control. The musicians were children in many ways, but once they became exposed to band life, any innocence that remained was soon consumed by the demands of their contracts, their bosses, and the record companies. Everybody wanted a piece of the action and a piece of Miller's powerful presence in the music world.

Tex Beneke, offers this insight:

> It was a very tough regiment, let me tell you. Wherever we went (Ray and the band), there was a fleet of cabs waiting outside for us simply because we had so little time between engagements. We might have, for instance, done a Chesterfield Broadcast and a few shows at the Paramount Theater in the morning ... in the afternoon, perhaps, cut a side or two at the studio ... go to the Café Rouge at

the Hotel Pennsylvania for several shows that evening and back for another Chesterfield show that night. Ray would grab his music off the stand, as would the rest of us guys, and stuff the music into the bell of our horns only to dash for the cabs with their instruments right in their hands. Yes, we were busier than time allowed.

Ray had no trouble at all. He joined Glenn's band as a pro and exceeded the best of them. He just stepped in very naturally, as though he had always belonged there. During his time with Miller, Ray was voted most popular singer by Downbeat, Metronome, and Variety magazines. No doubt his being with the band made him very popular and I believe he maintained it, too. Ray's voice just sounded better and better as he got older.

You know, Ray worked very hard, as did the rest of us, but I can tell you that none of us, including Ray, knew we were making history. The schedule, sometimes, was more than bearable, but we were unaware of the importance of that era.

Ray was very dear to me. He was a wonderful singer and he was one of those fellows I was proud to have known.

Dad's popularity with the band grew quickly. Glenn's band began recording all of those romantic ballads, and Dad's singing mixed with the great instrumentals the band played. They started recording on the Bluebird label, which was RCA's budget-priced label. One of the earlist songs my father recorded was "My Reverie" (9/27/38). This particular song had also been recorded by Bea Wain, who sang for Larry Clinton's band. It was actually very popular for Bea and Larry and she sang a smooth, sultry version of it that made a better impression than Dad's. He was just starting out and the early records and performances reflected that. He possessed a stark, smooth quality that was pure, youthful and unafraid. He kept working hard and tried desperately to please Miller. Most young men his age would have taken their celebrity and let it go to their heads. He was no exception.

He was a healthy, gifted twenty-year-old young man and did it ever go to his head! People liked to jitterbug, but they loved dancing close to one of Dad's ballads. He stood at the microphone, closed his eyes and poured out the very best he had. Miller had an exceptional cast of arrangers working for him and it showed in the band's performances. The only thing my father didn't like was that some of those arrangements, although clearly his ballads, were written to flatter the band and as a result pushed the vocal keys way out of his range. The problem eased as my father's voice got lower and, as he gained popularity, Glenn changed some of the keys to suit him better.

Glenn used to joke, with asides to Dad, "Hey, Eberle, stay on key, will ya'?" Often followed by, "And he doesn't sing too far behind the beat either."

The band's performances grew increasingly more frequent due to their extraordinary popularity. The aura that encircled Miller's organization was truly a phenomenon, and Miller's surge in popularity made other bands seem at a standstill. That's not to say that no other band was popular: they were all popular. Glenn's crew was, well, on fire and for the time it seemed surreal. Hotels and ballrooms wanted Glenn's band exclusively, and in addition to the usual agenda there were also live broadcasts. Chesterfield cigarettes sponsored something called the "Chesterfield Broadcasts" which gave the Miller band precious airtime and generated an increased popularity. The band was also doing Armed Forces Radio Transcriptions with spots advertising prophetically that "government war bonds were the only smart investment."

My father and Glenn were finally getting to know each other. Suddenly, for no apparent reason, Glenn began calling my father Jim. It caught on and later even my mother called him Jim. Dad asked him why he called him that and Glenn just told him he looked like a Jim. Around the same time Glenn began introducing Dad as "The Young Man in the Romance Department." Indeed, he was.

Glenn began taking my father under his wing, but not before delivering a check to his ego. One night, Glenn had recorded a live broadcast, as he routinely did, for educational purposes. That night the band sounded mildly ratty, and my father was letting every ballad rip as though he was the greatest of achievers. After the show, they all went to Glenn's room and listened to it. It was an embarrassment, and my father was humiliated. Glenn wasn't terribly mad, however and he took Dad aside. With compassion, he told Dad to work on his breath control so that he wouldn't leave a thought in the song dangling. He also taught him the importance of marrying the lyrics and music of a song together. Dad began to realize the importance of "telling the story," and his work improved noticably.

Once my father got over acting like a conceited, pompous brat who thought he'd put Bing Crosby right out of business, his relationship with Glenn grew both onstage and off. Sometimes Dad could hear Glenn mumbling under his breath while they were on stage. "Hey, Jim ... sing the words like they're written, will ya'?"

Life on the road was ever changing.

John Best, one of Glenn's trumpeters, relates the following.

> *Sometimes I'd ride with your Dad in the car between jobs. He was good company and we would cut up a lot. This one particular night, Ray and I had Dick Fisher, the guitarist, with us coming from a big affair in Boston. Well, we were merrily riding down a road in New England somewhere. To tease me, Ray would make a noise that sounded like a police siren and he'd startle me every time. He and Dick would laugh because I would look in the mirror and over my shoulder for the cops, only to realize I'd been fooled. A little later, I heard that confounded siren noise again and I turned to Ray and said, "You're not fooling me this time, smarty, with your sound effects!" Ray looked at me and said, "Well, it wasn't me ... honest!" We turned around and, sure enough, there were two cops in a car pulling us over. We heard one cop ask the other where we were from, as they glanced at my California plate. "Well, lock 'em up,"*

the other cop shouted. Dick Fisher, who was in the back seat, had a bottle of whiskey he was drinking and called them over to offer them some! And, they took it and we all stood around and talked and drank for a while ... then left!"

The fall and winter of 1938 were all about learning and many were burned out by the year's end.

The summer of 1939 however, was a fruitful time for the band. They were booked steadily at the Glen Island Casino in New Rochelle, New York and at Frank Daily's Meadowbrook Ballroom in New Jersey. The band hit the studio every few weeks, recording several tunes at each sitting. Many of those were Dad's ballads, some of which he'd never seen or heard before the recording session. He had the unpleasant task of learning the tune moments before laying down the track. There might be a little rehearsal time, but generally speaking, they went to the studio with the intention of recording takes.

That summer, Dad recorded "To You" and "Stairway to the Stars," and on August 1, 1939, the band recorded "In The Mood." On that particular day, they recorded six numbers in three hours. In addition to keeping up with their live perform-ances and broadcasts, Glenn's band managed to attend five recording sessions between October third and November twenty-second. In that time, eighteen tracks were laid down, eleven of them were my father's vocals, among them, "Indian Summer," "Faithful Forever" and, one of Glenn's personal favorites, "Blue Rain."

By this time, Dad and the band were beginning to shift into overdrive. Band members seldom had time for themselves, or for their families, or even for sleep. There was little time for any recreation of their own and many defaulted to drinking. People during that time drank a lot and musicians, stereotypi-cally, drank like the proverbial fish. My father was no excep-tion. He slept too little, ate too little and drank too much. It seemed to be the only way to relax. For members of the Miller Orchestra the day rarely ended before two in the morning or later, and they sometimes didn't return home until four or five in the morning. Sleep deprived night after night, the band often had to start their day around eight in the morning. Living like this week after week, or month after month takes its toll, as it did with my father. Little did he then know what he was doing to himself.

Toward the end of 1939, my father met my mother, Janet Young, at Frank Daily's Meadowbrook. My mother had entered a dance contest in which dancers competed to the music of Glenn Miller. Apparently, that night she caught my father's eye along with his hook, line and sinker. Before long, they were an item.

Janet had a daughter from a previous marriage, which ended quickly and was soon annulled by both sets of parents. Nancy (Atchison), Mother's beautiful daughter, was two when my parents met. Ray and Janet fell deeply in love; their friends knew it, their families knew it, the band knew it and Glenn knew it, too. One of the things that Glenn relied on was that Dad would flirt with the girls, bat his eyes and sing dreamily to them. Publicly, Glenn appeared happy about their love affair, but, in close circles, he wasn't happy at all at the prospect of his romantic male singer being "spoken for." Miller didn't make a big deal about other band members getting married, but he seemed a little threatened that his "Casanova" might be nesting down.

Ray and Janet were married in a private ceremony months later. She officially became an orchestra wife. Their life together spanned twenty-five years, surviving with strength, trust and undying love. Mother at first had trouble adjusting to life with an in-demand entertainer. And my father had his own tough issues, including being excommunicated from the Catholic Church because he had married a Protestant.

Chapter Three

After their marriage in 1940, Mother and Dad traveled, when necessary, together with Miller's band. When Dad performed within driving distance, my mother stayed in a small apartment nearby. Everyone loved my mother. The best way to describe her is that she was a determined woman, full of piss and vinegar and with a great head for business. Yet she was also warm, loving, unafraid and very smart. My mother was totally devoted to Dad and she was very involved in his career. She handled all the money, which was fortunate as it was one thing my father didn't do very well. Money always burned through Daddy's pocket; he spent it almost before he had it. Mom kept accounts balanced, their budget met and paid the bills. She also handled, along with his business affairs, his schedule, his suits, traveling and special appearances. As his career progressed, it was she who did his bookings and even advertisement. Mother believed in Dad all the way and proved to be not only a loving wife, but a wonderful asset to his growing career.

When celebrity first hit my father, he was wholly unprepared. In the theaters in particular, screaming girls, crowding around the stage and jitterbugging in the aisles, could leave him feeling like he didn't know what hit him. The situation was, however, usually more under control at the dance halls. By that time, Dad was making about fifty dollars a week. For all the work that entailed, it was better than his previous job and made clam-shucking a distant memory.

Paul Tanner, trombone player, Miller band member and friend reflects on this period:

When I joined Glenn's band in Atlantic City, New Jersey in the summer of 1938, your father was already with the band. I remember how much the ladies loved him. Ray's voice was still a little on the high side, but it lowered out quite nicely. I always thought he had such a good tone and quality to his voice and that he did a fine job on Miller's tunes.

Because I feel Glenn hired some of his musicians based on the fact that they had relatives who were talented and successful, I believe he hired your father for the same reason ... hopefully Bob Eberly's brother, Ray, would be as talented or better. Maybe he was hoping for good genes! In your father's case, Glenn turned out to be right.

There is one thing I can never forget about your father and that was his enormous strength! The man was as strong as an ox! It was always an ongoing thing that whenever anybody in the band needed something opened, they always called on Ray. It's funny, you know, one day I asked your father how he got to be so strong and he told me it was because he used to lift large barrels of beer at his father's hotel in Hoosick Falls. Can you imagine that?

Nineteen-forty was a very special year for Dad: he married his sweetheart, recorded some great tunes, was very busy and was voted the most popular singer in the country. And, at the end of the year, his first child, a daughter, was born. My sister's name is Raye Ellen.

Believe it or not, my father was the first to record a song that years later became extremely popular. "Blueberry Hill" was not a hit for Dad. Not even close, but his rendition rang out in the concert halls and ballrooms nonetheless. He also recorded one of my personal favorites, Eric Maschwitz and Manning Sherwin's 1940 composition, "A Nightingale Sang in Berkeley Square." That song would forever stay with him and would be one of the first tunes on which he recorded clearly his signature and style. The words to that song are so romantic and the music ... well ... a big cut above the rest of the songs he had been allowed to sing. Tex Beneke played one of his finest solos in that song.

> *That certain night, the night we met,*
> *There was magic abroad in the air.*
> *There were angels dining at the Ritz*
> *And a nightingale sang in Berkeley Square.*

Glenn Miller and his band were under contract in 1941 to perform in *Sun Valley Serenade*, their first feature film. The draws to the movie were skater Sonja Henie and actor John Payne. John replaced Dad in the picture because there was supposed to be a singer and it had to be the leading man. It was a film of fun and music and silly-nothing plots. While no one expected Dad to play the leading man role, he would've been valuable to the film. *Sun Valley Serenade* is about skiing, skating, kissing, falling in love and listening to dreamy music. I suppose that John and Sonja were needed to float the film, but Dad's singing was far better than John's. It was not the last time my father got the old shaft.

In 1942, the band filmed their second feature film titled, *Orchestra Wives*. This film was superior to the first—though it too was corny. The music was great and the lines were actually pretty funny at times. Besides Dad, Glenn, and the band, this film was chock full of stars and did not need floating.

Glenn Miller played a popular bandleader named Gene Morrison. George Montgomery played Gene's star trumpet player, a man with a history with women. Cesar Romero played his piano player and was the band's official playboy. And Jackie Gleason played Gene's bass player, a real family man. Jackie and Dad became good friends on and off the set. Their friendship began when Jackie walked up to Dad and announced he had a special gift for him. Jackie handed him a single match from a matchbook. After recovering from their laughter, my father reciprocated with something like a pebble. The next day, a grain of rice. The next, perhaps, a ball of lint. It was a good way to add some laughter to their hard work every day and after the film was finished, they remained good friends.

Two very good songs came out of that movie: "At Last" and "Serenade In Blue." Thankfully, both were my father's ballads, although for the film he shared the stage with a female singer and actress. She had a key role in the movie and, being a vocalist, it seemed the most natural spot for her. In the film, the character, known as Janey, played a troublemaker and manipulator *extraordinaire*. She had a villainous mind and twisted herself in and out of the lives of her onscreen friends. She bewitched band members and perplexed their wives. In general, her character brought the most zest to the picture. Those two songs, however, were Dad's ballads and, when Miller recorded them, they were Ray all the way! Billy May wrote the lengthy beginning to the record version of "Serenade in Blue," in and of itself a brilliant effort. Billy was a talented musician and very sweet man, but he was not a Miller fan and made no secret of it.

Orchestra Wives opens with the band, led by the fictitious "Gene Morrison," in the middle of recording their latest hit, "People Like You and Me." Everyone, except Janey, the female lead, is performing: Dad, Tex, Marion (who plays Ray's wife) and The Modernaires. After a successful cut, Janey walks into the studio, looking very smitten, and announces a secret. That secret is that Gene Morrison had booked the band on another grueling tour, after promising them a well-deserved vacation. As Gene enters the studio, the whole band meets him at the door and chants, "Roses are red, violets are blue, we're not going on a tour with you!" This scene is a little comical, but unfortunately, it was not all that far from the truth.

Orchestra Wives was complete by about the end of April 1942. My father and the band were looking forward to a vacation that had been promised to them by Glenn. Then, Glenn dropped the bomb, just as in the movie. He had betrayed the singers and band members by making a promise that he obviously had no intention of keeping. The band was going on a tour—and a long one—from Los Angeles back to Chicago, and on the way stopping at as many military bases as Glenn could possibly book. By then it became apparent, to at least some of the band members, that Miller, with the war upon them, wanted to do everything he could to get a military commission.

I have heard two speculations about Miller's motivations by members of his orchestra. One is that Glenn really was an ultra-patriot and wanted to contribute to the cause in any way that he could. The other was that Glenn gave up every chance at ballroom and dance affairs on this tour, a tour that would never have taken place if the band had gotten its way. The band was exhausted by the filming and wanted a break. Miller was pushing forty years old and many of the band members believed that Miller only wanted a commission for himself even if it was at the band's expense. This second version appears to be closer to the truth, though it pains me to say so, but I heard first-hand too much bitterness and resentment about this to surmise anything else. Miller was, indeed, a very shrewd businessman who between 1938–1942 made a lot of money off that civilian band. It certainly is in the realm of believability that, under the advice of other investors or businessmen in his organization, he was steered toward the possible benefits that a commission could afford.

I've heard many conflicting accounts surrounding this particular point in time, but most accounts agree that everyone was physically and mentally beat, and emotionally whipped, with little energy and little tolerance for each other. Band members were moody, crabby, overworked, and short-fused— including Glenn. According to one trombone player from his band then, Glenn was turned down by the Navy because of problems with his eyes, negotiated with the Army, and later ended up as a major in the Air Force.

The band arrived in Chicago after playing base after base all the way from Los Angeles. In Chicago they had nightly engagements at the Sherman Hotel as well as performing two live broadcasts from the Wrigley building three times a week: Tuesdays, Wednesdays and Thursdays. The first was for the East Coast and the second was for the West. At that time, everything was live and not pre-recorded. By the time the band got done with their evening engagement and headed over to perform the Pacific broadcast, many had been drinking. Needless to say, it was a very tough time. Getting from the Wrigley building to the Sherman Hotel necessitated that the band cross a bridge. If timed just right they could make it from the broadcast to the Hotel in time for the downbeat. However, hit the bridge at the wrong time and they got stuck waiting and couldn't make the Sherman on time. This all added to the pressure and tension on the band.

At about this time, my father told me there had been an ongoing dispute with Glenn concerning my dad's fee for his performance in *Orchestra Wives*. This dispute may have been a factor in my father's separation from Miller's organization. There has been much fascination and speculation regarding my father's divorce from Glenn Miller in 1942. Everyone seems to have an opinion, but no one has any answers. In rehashing every bit of information I ever received about this issue, fact or opinion, including my father's, I've concluded that my father was not fired. The most compelling evidence for this is that, for years, my father stated publicly and privately that he, in fact, had not been fired by Glenn. He maintained that he quit the band one morning after he arrived late for a rehearsal. I don't believe he'd planned to quit, but I think that morning things reached the breaking point. Certainly the combination of Dad's dispute with Glenn over his film fee and Glenn being tired and under tremendous pressure created a volatile situation.

As I stated earlier, Glenn had little tolerance for the drinking scene, especially in his band. And along with many others my father was caught drinking, though I don't know if he missed a job because of it. On the morning Dad strolled into rehearsal late, Glenn was furious. Both men were angry and shouting. Others claim to have witnessed the argument, yet no one can say for sure what it was about and whether they actually heard Glenn fire Dad. I specifically asked those I was able to contact and there was not one definitive "yes" in the bunch. There were many conflicts between Glenn and Dad. It's possible that Glenn knew my father's popularity was climbing rapidly and that may have threatened Miller in some way. At the same time he was pissed at my father and may have taken the opportunity to terminate his services.

It's plausible, but I believe my father quit the band that day in the heat of the moment. With his recording of "At Last," and "Serenade in Blue," and with his having been voted most popular singer in the country three times in succession, Dad was coming into his own and definitely on his way.

Chapter Four

In 1942 my father was twenty-three years old and, already, he had accomplished much. The four years prior had been a roller coaster of traveling, fame, recording sessions, fans and marriage. Finally, the train pulled up to the platform. Everything was still and quiet. Suddenly, everything came to a momentary stop.

Dad told me once that he was disappointed that things worked out the way they had with Miller; anger had faded to regret and, finally, to sadness. Even though Glenn had been a strong disciplinarian, Dad grew close to him. They didn't see eye to eye on everything, but their history meant something to Dad. He was young and vulnerable when he began with Glenn, but then, that's what Miller wanted. It's far easier to train and mold someone with little experience in your business than fighting to undo old habits. And, as a result of Dad's time with Miller, he became the kind of singing star others dream of becoming. Miller and my father did *each other* a favor by their teaming up together. Glenn went to bat for Dad at the beginning when others had their doubts. That was now all over.

Glenn went on into the Air Force. He tried getting his whole band into the service as one unit, but the military branches simply would not allow it. He offered a few of his choice men financial backing to start bands of their own. Most didn't make it. Tex Beneke refused his offer because he felt he just wasn't ready. After Glenn's attempt at relocating his civilian band, he knew he had no choice but to disband. It was after he disbanded that the military changed its view of whole bands being transferred overseas. So Glenn formed his Army Air Force Band, which included a string section, and went on to make a mark of its own.

Perry Como, singer, friend, and godfather to Ray, Jr. remembers:

> *I didn't look too far outside the small outfit I was with, but I certainly knew Glenn Miller's band was a huge success and that your Dad was one of the top three singers in the country at that time. Everyone*

knew that. When he was with Miller, we actually used to talk a lot about the road or arrangements we were singing at the time. Your Dad would say something like, "Boy, this new tune I'm doing is a toughie ... it's too high and the band is so loud you can't even hear me!" It was a hard life then and very hard work. I admired him for that.

Ray was a good friend and we used to talk about a great many things, especially in the band days. Ray was a great singer and was an extremely nice man who was well liked. He was also a great humorist who could always get a laugh! No one really realized the immensity of the Big Band Era or the impact of Glenn's disappearance. After Glenn, I always thought your father deserved more.

Word of Dad's leaving Miller's organization traveled swiftly. My father had continued to work in New York for a short period of time when he received an offer from Universal Studios, in Hollywood, to appear in several motion pictures. For the first time, he would be portraying himself—and with a new twist: *he* would be playing a bandleader.

A few of these films starred a very young Donald O'Conner, then a teen heartthrob who also did an awful lot of fabulous singing and dancing. Most of the plots were easygoing, mostly following plots of teen-like dreams, fame, love, wealth, love, love ...

Dad's immediate state of employment concerned him because he had a wife and children to support—and he was in New York. The movie studio was some three thousand miles due west. Then an interesting opportunity presented itself. Gene Krupa, who had drummed for some time with Benny Goodman, had broken off and formed a band of his own. Gene was not only very talented, but also quite together with his own organization.

Gene liked Dad's singing and reputation in the business and, no doubt, heard about the Eberle/Miller split. Krupa had a reputation of doing what he could to help other fellow artists in need. Temporarily, Dad fit that bill and Krupa offered him a job. My father certainly wasn't starving, but he knew he had to make things work and was eager to establish some long-standing plans and commitments. So my father took Gene up on his offer and became his new male vocalist. At that time, Gene's band included vocalists Anita O'Day, Charlie Ventura and Roy Eldridge, all three real musical personalities on their own. My father rounded out this feisty combination nicely. Joining Gene's band was really good for him because he received a great deal of respect and he felt free to relax and be himself. For the first time, Dad was really *with* a group of musicians. Dad and Gene became pretty good friends. They admired and respected each other a great deal and Gene also seemed part of the band rather than just the bandleader. He was one of the guys.

Between the end of 1942 and January 1943, my father toured with the great Gene Krupa and his crew. An album of various live broadcasts of that period gives a glimpse into the potpourri performances the group played. My father had historically been known as a great balladeer, but he stepped a little outside his old lines for Gene. He sang, among other things ,a sort of gospel-styled version of an old tune called "Praise the Lord and Pass the Ammunition," performed far from his style with Miller. And he also performed one of Helen Forrest's hits, "I Had the Craziest Dream," including the verse often overlooked in interpretation by other singers.

He had a good time with Krupa, pouring himself into dreamy versions of "Moonlight Mood" and "I Heard You Cried Last Night," rounding out an eclectic selection of tunes with a relatively conservative version of "Moonlight Becomes You." He remained close to his tradition, but the little bit of release was enough to give him a new taste of his own artistry and inside he knew there was much more than he had used with Miller.

My father spent a fairly short time with some of the best and brightest stars in his business. What can I say about the incomparable Anita O'Day? She is a queen among singers. And the pizzazz and energy of Roy Eldridge, Charlie Ventura and Remo Biondi were outstanding. Charlie was the leading white tenor sax man in the 1940's—with the possible exception of Tex Beneke. He was on fire and no other big band showcased the guitar like Gene did with Remo Biondi in this

1942-43 band. In June 1943, Gene disbanded what many feel was his greatest band, a band that also included Buddy DeFranco, Dodo Marmarosa, Teddy Penderson, and Johnny Bothwell. What a ride indeed!

By the time Gene and the crew arrived in California, my sister, Nancy had become the recipient of piano lessons from none other than Gene himself. It was informal: some basic piano lessons in return for some of my mother's spaghetti for dinner—more than a fair exchange. My father's time with Gene's outfit helped him to mature both personally and as an entertainer. At the very least, it tested his ability to adapt to a very different scenario. Gene's band was a little wild and quite fiery, while Miller's outfit had been more traditional and molded. I was told by a few of Miller's band members that Dad and Glenn had the opportunity to make amends before he left New York. Apparently, they ran into each other in New York and Glenn invited my father to join him, at an engagement in town, as a guest star. It was probably one of Daddy's more relaxed performances with Glenn because, in a way, the pressure was off. I know their reconciliation meant a lot to Dad because, despite their fierce blow-up, Dad still loved Glenn. That night was the last time Dad ever saw Miller.

Things in New Jersey were quite a bit different. Mother was busy packing and arranging for their trip West. The Eberles were Easterners, so adjusting to a visit West would be a challenge. Ultimately, they were never really able to call it home. Dad rented a house in Beverly Hills on Roxbury Lane that was convenient to the studio. It was a totally different life than he was used to. By then, my father was just really becoming aware of himself as a personality outside of the Miller outfit. He was a star all on his own, his hard work with Glenn having paid off. Singing was really the only thing my father knew how to do. While his life in Hoosick Falls may have stayed in his heart, music was in his soul and was his constant companion and he felt it would be for a long time.

Billy May remembers:

When Ray signed with Universal Studios to make those five pictures, they (Dad and Janet) move to Los

Angeles. In fact, I remember the house they rented was down the street from Lana Turner—it was 519 Roxbury Lane. And, I remember your older sisters Raye Ellen and Nancy being there. I can recall your Uncle Bob would come to visit. Ray and Bob would love to play tricks on Janet. They would go in the other room like they were talking long distance to Hoosick. They'd pretend they were talking to all their aunts, uncles, cousins and anyone else in town they could find. I would hear them say things like, "Can I talk to Uncle Charlie now? What? Oh, he's down at the barber's? Well, that's O.K. ... we'll hold on while you get him!" Bob and Ray would take turns going in and out of the room pretending to talk long distance. Janet would be furious and worry about the huge phone bill!

After settling into their new home, my family continued on with a fairly normal life. My sisters went to school and it didn't take long for them to make friends. My parents became fast friends with a woman who lived down the street from them on Roxbury. Her name was Lana Turner. The area they all lived in made life easier because of its proximity to the movie studios. It's bad enough having to wake every morning before sunrise, but if you had a long morning drive to the studio it could be miserable. The friendship with Lana grew and my father impishly admitted he attended a costume party at Lana's dressed as Huckleberry Finn. Lana, in fact, took to my father so much that she gave him a dog. I don't know if he was just too much for her to handle or if she actually shopped it for him, but it was not just the average dog. The dog bordered on being horse size. I'm not sure what his name was, but my father really grew to love the dog.

One day, my father and "the horse" were driving through Beverly Hills in his convertible and were waiting at a traffic light on Sunset Boulevard. Also sitting at the intersection were two officers in their patrol car, waiting to catch some unsuspecting speeder. Dad's dog used to like sitting in the passenger's seat so that he could experience the full effect of the convertible ride. Nothing beats a dog's drooling jowls flapping in the breeze. As Dad and his companion sat next to the patrol car, the dog being ever so curious, looked to his right to inspect the officer, who sat only inches away. The unsuspecting officer turned his head slowly to the left only to find himself face to face with the monstrous, slobbering head of a Great Dane. The officer jumped and hit his head on the roof of the patrol car. The light changed, Dad put the car in gear laughing to himself as he continued down Sunset Boulevard.

Nineteen forty-three turned out to be a busy year for my father; no longer owned by one man, not exclusive to one orchestra, he was free to explore new possibilities. Besides beginning his movie career with Universal Studios, he enjoyed going into the recording studio to record transcriptions, used over the radio for weekly broadcasts that were directly for the benefit of the "men and women of the armed forces." Each week a celebrity was chosen to fulfill requests, which were interrupted with some monologue written by the radio producers. This way the servicemen had a chance to hear their request dedicated directly to them by singing stars they loved. These sessions were done mainly with piano accompaniment only. That can be a challenge for those used to being able to hide behind a full orchestra designed to flatter the singer. With only a piano, there is no place to hide.

Those recordings captured some of my father's best singing—maybe not the fanciest and most glamorous, but it was stark and pure and his voice was unhidden. And it was during this time that Dad recorded one of the best versions of "That Old Black Magic," with only a piano accompaniment.

Between touring with Gene's band early in 1943 and working on several pictures at Universal Studios, Dad had little time for anything extra on his plate. That included his enormous amount of fan mail from many parts of the world that he had been getting since leaving Miller. Once more my mom stepped in answering some of the fan mail on his behalf, sending mostly personal, handwritten letters to them all after reviewing them with Dad.

One such fan letter came from a teen in South Africa. His name was Noel Swart. He was an avid fan of Dad's and requested my father be an honorary member of his club. My mother answered his letter on November 1, 1943.

Dear Noel Swart:

Mr. Eberle was very much interested in your letter and wanted me to answer this personally for him.

As you no doubt know, the Glenn Miller Orchestra has disbanded and Glenn is now a captain in the Army Air Corps. Some of the band boys are in the service now and the rest are pretty much scattered around the country. As Ray is the father of two little girls, he hasn't received "the call" as yet. Ray is under contract to Universal Studios and he has made several pictures in the past nine months. Have they come to South Africa as yet? If you'd like to see Ray, some of the titles of the pictures are as follows, Follow the Band, Mr. Big, This is the Life, Three Cheers For the Boys, *etc...*

Your club sounds very interesting and I know Ray would feel honored to be considered an honorary, inactive member of your club.

She closed this letter thoughtfully and proudly signed, Mrs. Ray Eberle for Ray Eberle. In 2001, through unusual happenstance, I found myself in contact with Noel Swart who still had my mother's letter from 1943. Knowing I had few personal effects of my mother's, this unselfish, generous man put this letter into my possession. What a thrill it was for me to see, fifty-eight years after it was written, my mother's handwritten words.

Some of the movies Dad was under contract to perform in were: *Follow The Band* (1943), *Mr. Big* (1943), *This Is The Life* (1944), *Hi'ya Sailor* (1943), and *Honeymoon Lodge* (1943). They included such stars as Donald O'Connor, Peggy Ryan, Gloria Jean, Eddie Miller's Bobcats, Elyse Knox, Wingy Manone and Ozzie and Harriet Nelson. Shortly after he'd completed a few films, he received a draft notice from the Army and was to report to a base in North Carolina. Dad served for the remaining eighteen months of World War II, after which he promptly returned to my mother and his life as a civilian and a singer. He was anxious to resume his work in clubs and movies.

During his time in the Army, he experienced the major loss of his young life. My father told me about the day he heard the news about Glenn Miller's disappearance over the English Channel while in a flight from England to France. It was a cold morning in December and he was so jolted by the news and its reality that he was in denial for days. For many of that era, it paralleled the pain of the murder of John Lennon in front of his New York City apartment or the sudden deaths of Princess Grace or Princess Diana. Dad loved Glenn and he felt that loss for the rest of his life.

Upon returning to California after serving eighteen months in the Army, my father started receiving bookings to appear with his new band, "The Ray Eberle Orchestra." He also completed any contractual responsibilities he had with Universal Studios. Now twenty-six, his professional and personal lives were now both fulfilling and memorable. The family's stay on the West Coast extended a little longer, but eventually they arranged for their return to the Northeast. It was the place they most loved. Family roots were important to Mother and Dad and they tried hard not to lose sight of that. Things around the house were usually fairly "normal," with the exception of prominent people who visited their home on occasion. Whether it was Krupa to give a piano lesson, Cesar Romero for a plate of my mother's spaghetti, or Lana Turner for a neighborly chat, my mother always managed to keep the "show-biz" stuff out of the house. And the pictures of Dad's performances on the walls? Oh, those were just pictures of Dad at work.

Dad was still the boy from Hoosick Falls. He loved his family and fishing and, when he wasn't working, puttering around the house. My father's career was going pretty well at that time, though the concern that he wasn't schooled in anything else remained with him. He felt he sang in part because he didn't know what else to do. Daddy had become a respected entertainer in the business, but continued concentrating on what he couldn't do, and it restricted to an extent his ability to enjoy his early stardom.

The Eberles returned East and settled a short distance from New York City, in New Jersey. He was now back doing personal appearances and playing dates with his new band. His life began rolling forward again and *the train* was leaving yet another station, continuing to gain momentum. The husband, father and singer were still searching for who they really were.

And the train rolled on.

Circa 1941 - Glenn, announcer Larry Bruff, Paula Kelly, and Dad working on music and script for a show.

Chapter Five

With the formation of his band, in the mid 1940's, my father worked quite a bit and traveled on a regular basis. When he wasn't traveling, he occasionally found home on a few sound stages performing in what were once called "shorts" or "shorties"; the music videos of the 1940's and 1950's. Shorts ran anywhere from an average three minute song to as long as fifteen or twenty minutes: they were short versions of a film.

My father did a few shorts, but there was one in 1946 that particularly strikes me as "Ray." The scene is a beautiful garden on a sunny day in the park. There are gorgeous flowers about and a romantic gazebo streaming with greens and vines. In front of the gazebo sits a white Adirondack style bench for two. The elaborate, romantic music begins and my father and a woman stroll into the picture. In the film, they are obviously in love. Dad stares romantically into the woman's eyes and begins to sing this tune: *"Everything I have is yours, you're part of me..."* Needless to say, he spends the next three minutes proclaiming his love to her, promising her the moon and the stars and all that he has. Finally, they are seated on the bench. He slips a ring onto her finger and at the end of the tune, validates all he has proclaimed with a romantic kiss. "Everything I Have Is Yours," was a perfect match for my father.

I sometimes wonder whether or not Dad would have formed his own band at all if he had not done the pictures at Universal protraying himself as a real bandleader. Perhaps it was a natural progression for him. Members of Dad's band tell me they liked him as a boss. They especially liked his sense of humor, and of course, his voice. His band played many well-known tunes that were arranged nicely, and the caliber of musicians he hired was top. They weren't all Jazz musicians but they all appreciated good arrangements and the opportunity to play in good clubs. At one point later in his career, my father hired a young Chick Corea, though the relationship didn't last long.

Work was good and plentiful enough for Dad to consider expanding the Eberle family once again. Nancy was now a teenager, and Raye Ellen was not far behind. They were excited at the thought of having a new baby sister or brother, and while adjustments had to be made for once again having a baby in the house, my mother and father so loved children that it was never an *adjustment* to them.

In September of 1953, Laurie Ann joined the Eberle family. She has Dad's dark features, deep brown eyes and dark brown hair. Her hair color was reminiscent of Grandma Margaret's. Raye and Nancy, in sharp contrast, had light hair and a fair complexion. We all have the "Eberle" cleft on our chins from Dad, and a thin European nose from Mother. After having Laurie, my mother developed fibroid tumors in her uterus so at 34 it was unclear if she would be able to have any more children.

The 1950's were, no doubt, the best and busiest times for Ray Eberle and his Serenade in Blue Orchestra. Most of the traveling he did was on the road with the band. He rarely had reason to fly anywhere unless, perhaps, he was needed on a sound stage in California for a short or walk on in a picture. The band traveled well in three or four large-sized cars, loaded up with luggage, music and instruments. My father owned a new DeSoto station wagon and was able to get a lot of people and band equipment in there. Bernie Fox, who played tenor sax and became Dad's road manager, remembered that car fondly. My father used to let Bernie drive it and they often traveled together.

One of the things Bernie remembered was my dad's fondness for giving gifts. Around Christmas time, Dad bought the band members travel clocks or Scotch plaid stadium blankets and little knick-knacks to let the guys know just how much he appreciated them. When Bernie and his wife, Bea, got married, he bought Bernie a Black & Decker crosscut saw because he knew how much he enjoyed building furniture. Bernie talked very fondly about being part of Dad's band and he shared with me wonderful memories from that part of his life.

One night, my father and the band were doing a job at a country club. After about every forty or forty-five minutes, the guys took a break for a drink and a smoke. This one particular evening, Ray had been a little on the quiet side. Bernie and another sax player, Bert Kosow, decided to join Dad in the garden for a cigarette to keep him company. The three men stood next to each other for several moments without saying a word. Finally, my father spoke.

"Bonnie ran away," Dad mumbled quietly. Bert and Bernie looked on with concern.

"Is that the big one or the little one?" replied Bert.

"The big one or little one what?" Dad's eyes grew large.

"One of your girls has run away?"

My father quickly figured out what they were talking about and burst into uproarious laughter.

"Bonnie is my dog!"

The guys in the band never forgot the "Bonnie" joke and never let Bert and Bernie live it down.

A lot of funny things happen when you are together with a group of people every day for long periods of time. One evening, the band was playing a very crowded dance. People used to approach my father all night to talk and get autographs or have a laugh or two with him. And he loved interacting with fans and met a great many interesting people that way. This night, an older gentleman, perhaps twice my father's age of thirty-nine, walked up.

"Hi," said the old man, "do you remember me?"

Dad looked at his elder and thought a moment. He met so many people everyday that it was hard for him to remember any one person. While Dad was thinking, some of the band members were standing around with him and heard the old man's question. Finally, my father replied politely.

"No, I don't think so ..."

The old man continued.

"No? We went to school together!"

Well, my father was barely half this man's age and the guys in the band were absolutely relentless when it came to teasing my father.

Bert Kosow relates this road trip story:

> *I remember we played an Air Force base down in Panama City, Florida and it was a real fishing town. It*

was the first time I'd played there, but your father played there a number of times before and, while at the Air Force base, he told me how much he loved to fish. He said there was a bridge over an island or that there was somewhere he said you could go out onto the bridge, drop a line and you could just have a ter-rific day fishing. Now, I have to tell you that I've never been keen on fishing. I fished lakes out in Minnesota and have friends who have taken me out to Long Island Sound and I never really enjoyed it. So, Ray said to me, "Come on, I'm going to take you out fish-ing with me (tomorrow) and we're going to have a good time." And I said, "Ray, forget it. I really don't want to go." Somehow, we ended up staying awake all night and there were about four of us and we were just sitting around talking ... talking musician stories. It was just one of those times when we just felt like staying up.

The next night, we were playing one of those places that was not too far away ... it was kind of a short trip. Anyway, I told Ray "no" to fishing and that I'd rather go to sleep and, I said, "Quite frankly, I don't know how to tell you this, but I have a liaison with a young lady tomorrow morning. She told me to pick her up after church." Anyway, I told Ray I wasn't going fishing with him. It got to be around five-thirty or six in the morning. The sun was up. Ray said, "C'mon, let's go down and we'll just drop a line off the bridge for an hour or two." Finally, I said, "Alright. Let's go."

And the other fellows were kind of keen, so we went down and there were all these fishing shacks where you could rent fishing equipment because we didn't have any with us. I remember we got down to the shack and Ray started talking to the owner of the shop about rods and reels. The man said, "You know, this fishing boat right here is getting ready to go out now. Why don't you go out on this boat?" And Ray said, "No, we can't do that because we have to be back. We can't spend the whole day away." The man replied, "Well ... they're only going out for an hour or two." Well, your father turned to us and said, "How about it?" I said, "Ray, you said you wanted to go to the bridge for an hour or two and that would be it." He grinned at me and said, "But, the boat is going out for an hour or two and it'll be fun!"

The next thing I know, we are all on the boat and the boat is pulling away from the shore. One of the fellows, Al Thompson, turned around to one of the mates on the boat and asked, "What time are we coming back today?" And the mate replied, "Six." Al said, "A.M.?" The mate looked at him strangely and answered, "No! P.M.!" Well, in the first place, we all got sick. We didn't catch any fish, but I think your father had a very good time. By the time we got back, it was a scramble to get ourselves together for the next job.

That night, on the bandstand, Ray got up to sing a song called, "P.S., I Love You." He was standing in front of the microphone and he was standing right in front of my music stand. The first line of the song goes, "Dear, I thought I'd drop a line ..." And, I said in a stage whisper, "... over the bridge, just for an hour or two!" He could not sing the next sixteen bars ...

There was also the occasional tearful curve. At the beginning of the new year of 1958, Dad's band was pretty popular at the service bases, colleges, and private dances. The official *big band era* was over, but they remained very successful and my father had maintained his popularity by trying to keep his music fresh and his band happy. At about this time, Bernie had taken ill with heart problems and told my father that he wouldn't be allowed to play for a while. He suggested to Dad that he approach Bert Kosow to take his place as road manager because he knew Bert could handle it. Bert stepped in as road manager and continued to play his tenor sax as well.

The band was due to start a string of jobs in what seemed to be a confusing order, unconnected in their proximity; sometimes dates just happen to fall that way. There was a lot of driving involved and the band by now had it down to a science. Dad and his band members met in Manhattan at about six o'clock in the morning to discuss their plans. Six o'clock in the morning is the middle of the night to a musician, so the thought of a long drive that day was not relished. Once assembled they all left New York City bound for Augusta, Georgia— at least a twelve hour drive.

Later that evening, two of the three cars arrived at the hotel with just enough time to clean up and set up the stage for their ballroom affair. The third car finally arrived carrying four members of the band and their female singer. The driver and bass player, Phil Calasemo, Sal Carbone, who played trombone, Phil's singer/wife, Susan, their drummer Mel Zelman and finally tenor sax man, Jack Sommers. Jack was Bernie's replacement. Phil walked into the hotel and began talking to Bert. He started explaining that he didn't want to check in that night because he planned to drive on to the next job after that night's show.

"I don't think that's a very good idea, Phil. I think you should just get a good night's sleep and not worry about saving a few bucks for a hotel room."

Bert seemed concerned about Phil's intentions. Phil was a quiet and reserved type of fellow. He went and brought over a couple of the other fellows who were in his car that said they really wanted to go on to the next job, which happened to be at an Army base in Marianna, Florida. Sal Carbone, who had known Bert for many years, was one of the men in Phil's car. Bert and Sal were in the Army together and while they hadn't grown up together they had a certain bond. Sal began negotiating with his friend, the road manager.

"Look, Bert, everyone feels great and we want to go ... really."

Bert challenged his friend.

"It's really foolish. Why do you want to drive at night? We just got here from a very long haul and to tell you the truth, I thought the band looked tired when they got here. Now that the job is over, I *know* everybody is beat."

They were all so insistent and Bert kept trying to talk them out of it, but he relented. They all wanted to go to Marianna.

"I'll tell you what I'll do," Bert said matter of factly, "if everyone in the car agrees they *all* want to go on, then I can't stop you. I can't order you not to go. But, if one of you hesitates to go in the least, then you all have to stay."

They all approached Bert one last time and unanimously agreed to make the trip that late night in January. Bert agreed, but had reservations.

"O.K., but Phil ... please be careful because you are tired, you know. Don't take anything or drink anything. Just take it easy, man."

Phil smiled at his friend one last time before pushing off for Marianna.

"No problem. We all feel great and we'll be fine, O.K.?"

The rest of the band retired for a good night's sleep and planned to enjoy a more leisurely drive the next day.

My father and the remaining members of his band left the next morning bound for Marianna, Florida. Bert, as usual, was driving Dad's DeSoto. It was a warm, beautiful day in Florida and Ray and Bert enjoyed their relaxing drive to the base. Finally, a short time later, they pulled up to the gatehouse of the military installation and stopped to check in with the guard. The band was set to play a dance at the officer's club that evening and it was necessary to check in. Dad and Bert enjoyed themselves so much that day, they were in great moods, laughing and joking as they stopped at the guardhouse. The officer on duty asked what their business was and my father explained who he was and the nature of their visit. When the guard heard that, his face dropped immediately and a grim look fell over him. He told them where to park the wagon and began to move away from them. Bert followed his instruction and pulled up to the officer's club. As my father got out of the car, someone instantly walked out toward him, not saying a word. They knew, at that point, something had to be wrong. The officer pulled Dad aside to talk to him and, at the same time, Rod Lewis, one of the sax players from a car that arrived before Ray's, began to talk to Bert.

"Rod, what's the matter?"

"Oh, God, Bert ..." Rod said in a nervous tone, "there's been a terrible accident. Bert, three of them didn't make it ..."

Bert was in shock and began speaking in a panicked tone.

"Phil? What about Phil?" Rod shook his head to indicate "no." "Oh, my God, and Sal? NOT SAL! No, not Sal ..."

Bert shook his head in disbelief, feeling his loss instantly.

Phil Calasemo, his wife/singer, Susan and Sal Carbone, who had all been seated in the front, were dead. Mel Zelman, who was seated behind the passenger's seat, sustained serious head injuries as part of his skull shattered. Jack Sommers, who sat behind Phil, amazingly enough suffered only a broken arm and some other non-life threatening injuries.

After the initial shock, Dad and Bert were escorted into the officer's club and were given a drink to help them calm down. My father was a basket case. He cared deeply for those people who had shared so much of their lives with him and he felt helpless because there was nothing he could do to bring them back. They were gone forever. As they sat at the bar, the rest of the details were revealed to Dad and his road manager.

There was an eyewitness who was driving a passenger bus behind Phil's car. According to the bus driver, they had been going along just fine. Phil hadn't been speeding, weaving or driving irresponsibly in any way. Coming in the opposite direction, however, was a car that swerved and hit the band car head-on at a very high rate of speed. The impact killed the three unsuspecting band members instantly. The strange thing about all of this is that Bert and my father had passed the accident that morning in the early part of the trip. The car was off the road with police tape around it, so badly damaged that it was unrecognizable to Bert as Phil's car which normally was easily recognized because it was distinctive and sort of flashy with its stripes and other markings. But, to Dad and Bert, that morning in too good a mood to notice, it was just another car that wrecked on the side of the road.

This terrible news hit everyone like a giant shock wave. That day was also my father's thirty-ninth birthday. He was devastated, but they had to play the job that night. There wasn't enough time to arrange otherwise. Dad contacted the local musician's union in a desperate attempt to replace the people he had lost and lucked out in finding men to fill the empty band seats.

As Bert set up the bandstands and waited for the substitutes to arrive, he stared sadly at the stands that contained the closed black music books. Daddy sang alone that night; perhaps reality was setting in.

Co-workers, friends—were gone in an instant. My father and his band were spinning with sorrow and anger.

That night stretched out like no other. When the dance was over, my father wanted the subs to receive their pay immediately for making such an effort on such short notice. He was so upset he could barely sign his name on the checks. Musicians who had filled in that night all then went to my father and tore up their checks, refusing to accept payment for the work they had done out of respect for my father and the band's loss. They were men who all knew what it was like to be part of something together, one man of many, creating one sound. The *esprit de corps* was amazing. Strangers that appeared so suddenly and then disappeared. As for his three friends, they were gone forever.

Chapter Six

Glenn Miller is a legend, but so, too, are his songs and singers. Consequently, it was natural that Dad, Paula (Kelly) and The Modernaires banded together with Tex for the formation of the Miller Singers reunion.

Tex had led the Glenn Miller Army Air Force Band after the war, but eventually broke his contract with Helen Miller and the Miller organization, claiming that he could barely make ends meet with an orchestra of its size. After his contractual relationship was over with the Miller estate, he formed his own band and played *in the Glenn Miller style.*

To the best of my personal knowledge, Tex Beneke's band was not totally, officially sanctioned by the Miller estate, but were nevertheless not prevented from performing in the Miller vein. My father, Tex, Paula and The Mods banded together to present *the guts* of the Miller phenomena. It is where I believe the heart was and still remains.

Anyone who has watched the movie, *The Glenn Miller Story* (1954), might conclude that the exclusion of his most key band members from the movie looks a bit nonsensical. It would be no different than if one of the Beatles told his life story, including his success with the Beatles, and excluded the other members as though they simply were not a part of that point in history. I suspect both my father and Tex must have been hurt and miffed by that. The formation of the reunion group revealed the truths about how vital their participation in Glenn Miller's organization really was to the soul of Glenn's music, so to speak.

Just before the Glenn Miller singers reunited for this new ride, my father had the opportunity to participate in a television event on NBC titled, "Swing Into Spring," a musical show also starring Benny Goodman, Ella Fitzgerald, Harry James, the McGuire Sisters, Jo Stafford, and Teddy Wilson. It was an hour of fun and great music that reminded the audience how wonderful Swing music is and of its contribution to music history.

With the renewed interest in the big bands and in Glenn Miller in particular, Dad made a couple of albums in the late 1950's with his own band. *Ray Eberle Sings and Plays Music of Today* was an album in which he attempted to step outside the familiar "Ray" lines. The tunes were recorded in *the Glenn Miller way*, but "Elmer's Tune," and "Chattanooga Choo Choo" were done as Cha-Chas, while "My Blue Heaven" and "You Stepped Out of a Dream" were sung and played in Swing. It turned out to be a real finger-snapper. Dad's rendition of "Did I Remember" and "Stairway to the Stars" were really dreamy and his voice appeared to be getting better with age. He had matured and his voice had matured and he had the added luxury of selecting the key he wanted to record it in. The record was a nostalgic success.

Ray Eberle Plays Glenn Miller Favorites was another album he completed around this time and it included Dad's vocal on Glenn Miller's theme song, "Moonlight Serenade." It was a tune which was regularly performed when Tex, Dad, Paula and The Mods were doing the reunion shows. Other tunes included "Blue Champagne," "Skylark," "It's A Blue World," "Deep Purple," and an updated version of "At Last."

Paula Kelly, Jr. reflects on this time.

> *I first met your father in 1961 when I was still in high school. We had just moved from Tarzana. I walked into the house and heard hysterical laughter coming from one of the bedrooms. My father (Hal Dickinson from The Modernaires) was not a handy man by any stretch of the imagination, but he and Ray were trying to assemble a bed ... and doing a bad job! Together, they looked ridiculous! Neither man looked like handy men to me! How the bed ever got assembled I'll never know.*
>
> *Ray mentioned many times that Glenn was a real disciplinarian. He was tough to work with and for and expected the very best from everyone involved with his outfit. Life was tough and the work was hard, but Glenn was fair.*

The Eberle Named Ray

Your Dad, Tex, and The Modernaires went to Europe in the 1960's and recorded a number of albums during that time, too. They all did their best and were loved by many people. My parents (Hal Dickinson and Paula Kelly of The Modernaires) did the Bob Crosby Show in the 1950's and nightclubs when their schedules allowed. All and all, I think everything was O.K. Who knows what might have been. They were great together and your father was a special man and a great singer. Ray was a joy to be with and I miss him very much. He was a funny guy with a heart of gold. He was also like a brother to both of my parents and I know that meant a lot to them.

The family was living in Short Hills, New Jersey by the late 1950's. That house took almost two years to build and was passionately designed by my father, and included lowered counters in the bathrooms for my mother, who was less than five feet tall. Actually, it made sense as everyone in the family was short. The house was four bedrooms with a sunken living room and a beautiful whitewashed brick fireplace in the living room. The kitchen was long and sort of galley style and my father had a paneled den.

My mother and father built their dream house and his career continued successfully. The children were all happy and growing, and Mom and Dad were enjoying a second honeymoon phase of their marriage. They were traveling a lot, enjoying the sightseeing and laughs. They were both forty and their life together had survived over two decades. Then quite suddenly they received bittersweet news. God was blessing them with one more child—but my mother was diagnosed with cancer.

The doctor was unsure what my mother's options would be. Here was a forty-year old woman who was pregnant and, at the same time, was expected to fight what was then referred to as "Type A" cancer. This particular cancer was vicious and unpredictable; like a wildfire it could flare in one part of the body and jump to another.

The cancer had my mother feeling out of control and she deserved better. She opted to go through with the pregnancy; for her, abortion was never an option. She refused cancer treatments while she was pregnant with me, fearing it would hurt the fetus. When the time was right, she would receive cobalt treatments. Her decisions were very unselfish.

Dad was expressive in ways that allowed him to create the kind of beauty he had with his voice, but Ray Eberle was not the sort of man who wore his heart on his sleeve. In our house, my mother shared her feelings a little and was empathetic to all, but she was a bit of a caretaker. As a group we didn't share feelings a lot. Everyone just sort of walked around grinning all the time as if the world was a giant lollipop and we were the suckers. We saw nothing, we heard nothing, and ... we said nothing. With my mother's illness and my father's increased drinking, tension began to mount. Nevertheless, life continued passing by like the rhythmic clicking of railroad ties.

But, my father's train had begun to move out of control.

By the time 1960 rolled around, my father was putting out at least one album per year with the reunion group, including one with Marion Hutton called *The Former Glenn Miller Singers*, but there was an incredible sadness in the air. My family knew exactly what cancer meant and the lack of rhyme or reason to this type of cancer baffled doctors who knew they couldn't stay ahead of it. It was difficult and unusual in 1960 for a woman over 40 to give birth. During her pregnancy, the cancer had parked itself in my mother's colon and was spreading to her uterus and rectum at a fairly fast pace. The only thing the doctor could do was to keep her comfortable.

The weeks and months of her pregnancy proved to be both painful and worrisome for Dad and Mother. The closer she came to delivery, the more concerned they became about the baby. There seemed a certain gratification, under the circumstances, to her for having just one more.

Her last child.

Her miracle child.

With my father playing dates with his own band and working new gigs with the reunion group, all eyes were on Mom. A few weeks before her due date, the doctor had to perform a colostomy. The urgency of her condition necessitated that they remove the baby in utero to do it. The procedure was unusual and was later written in medical journals. Imagine: take baby out, do a little thing, put baby back, sew her up!

Finally, on May 1, 1960, I made my first official appearance into this world, fortunate to be here in one piece: ten fingers and ten toes. Now my mother could concentrate on getting well. She decided that I would be her namesake and named me Jan. I am flattered to be named after someone with that much kindness and courage. As I have grown, I feel that I truly was the last living part of her, a new beginning.

In 1961, Warner Brothers Records, Inc. released their first album of the Glenn Miller singers titled, *Music Made Famous by Glenn Miller*. The live album starred Tex Beneke and his Orchestra, Ray Eberle, Paula Kelly and The Modernaires. The audience reaction, as clearly heard on the album, was more than rousing. They wanted more. This was it. This was the way things were supposed to be. Dad, Tex, Paula: they all felt it. The audience was really with them and they drank the juices of satisfaction.

My father told me later how scared they all were that night. Although they had been performing together in their reunion group for a couple of years, the album was the test of true acceptance. They asked themselves, "Would people remember? Would people react positively? Is this what they want?" Nostalgia, the point where history and love meet: this was the way things were supposed to be.

One of the things that happened in the music world during the late 1950's and 1960's was the development of big star shows in Las Vegas. Many singing stars found a new home in Vegas because of the caliber of casinos and nightclubs and the large audience they drew. Many singers who had come from the Big Band Era were now in demand as headliners in many of the casino nightclubs. It was the period of Frank Sinatra's arrival with his famed "Rat Pack." Frank was only one of many famous celebrities who took Vegas by storm and helped Las Vegas build a reputation for presenting first-class entertainment.

My father, Paula and Tex and his Orchestra were also beginning to frequent Las Vegas by 1962. Their fans stayed loyal and apparently Warner Brothers Records believed in them, too, because they released a second live album titled, *Music Made Famous by Glenn Miller: Silver Jubilee Album*. This event was recorded in the Casbah Theater at the Hotel Sahara and even more electrifying than their first live recording. People were pouring into their shows night after night, some standing on their chairs to applaud. The audiences were grateful for the memories that came flooding back with songs like "Tuxedo Junction," "Sunrise Serenade," "Sweet Eloise," "St. Louis Blues March," "Elmer's Tune" and "Don't Sit Under the Apple Tree." The familiar singers were seen on stage twenty years after their earlier careers, but their voices had matured, seasoned and ripened.

As I became a toddler, my mother spent more and more time at the doctor's office and was in bed more frequently. Dad was working a busy schedule with live record albums and appearances with both his Serenade In Blue Orchestra and the Miller Singers Reunion. I suspect being that busy for Dad then was a blessing and kept his mind off how sick my mother was becoming. He spent every moment with her when he was home, but when he wasn't, the rest of us rallied around her and a housekeeper smoothed things for us younger kids (Nancy and Raye Ellen were now married).

As I got a little older, my sister, Laurie, and I traveled more and more with Mom and Dad. We spent months at a time in Las Vegas. My mother loved Vegas, not for the casinos but for the therapeutic warm, dry weather. While Dad was busy rehearsing most afternoons, Mom, Laurie and I spent time at the pool. When Dad was with us, we enjoyed seeing the local rodeos and spent time with friends and family who came to visit us. Mother was starting to look thin and pale with very dark circles under her eyes. She always smiled at me, though, as she went about just being Mom.

My father's plans for 1963 were full. In March, he was scheduled to appear on "Perry Como's Kraft Music Hall," followed by another Warner Brothers record album in the fall. My father and Perry met back in the band days when Perry was with Ted Weems' Band and had remained in touch.

The cast that evening was impressive. Besides the reunion group, my father and Perry there was Carol Lawrence, and an appearance by Glenn Miller's niece, Wynn Miller. She was connected to a few Broadway musicals then, like, *Li'l Abner, A Thurber Carnival* and *Tenderloin*. There was a segment in the show in which Perry and Dad exchange dialogue and pictures of their grandchildren. It was humorous and reminiscent of their easy-going relationship, their commonalities in the business and their close-knit families. My oldest sister Nancy had married one of Perry's writers, John Aylesworth, and their child was one of the grandbabies they cooed over. At that time, I was only a few years older than my sister's children.

My father looked fit during the production of Perry's show in March of 1963, but the stress of my mother's illness was beginning to show. Dad's drinking increased greatly after going for many years with little drinking, following the serious drinking of his band days with Miller. Physically and emotionally, my father was only just holding together. As happens to people who consume abusive amounts of alcohol, Dad's body became allergic and his mind became addicted. My father was becoming an alcoholic.

There were no stops left on a train that was now running unattended, and his precious cargo—his wife, his children, his career and himself—were all along for the ride. Once you cross the line into the disease, you can never return. The disease offers no cure.

The seasons were coming full circle once again. Cold and empty was followed by spring and the hope of new life, then summer and the warmth of feeling alive. But, we were losing that warmth to the dying, gray sense of autumn. And, soon, winter would reveal its darkness and its death. My mother would not revel in her springtime lilies of the valley, nor would she bask in another summer sun.

My mother and me in June 1960.

top left: John (Grandpa Jack) Eberle in Mechanicville, New York, as a police officer - early 1900's.

top right: Mid 1920's, Hoosick Falls, NY. Dad (on right) aged 6 or 7 years, with a friend.

right: Hoosick Falls, NY, late 1920's. Ray (on left) and younger brother, Walter.

The Eberle Named Ray

1942 - The real Orchestra Wives taken during filming of Orchestra Wives. Back row, actors: George Montgomery, Cesar Romero, Jackie Gleason. My mother, Janet, is the blond in the center of the photo wearing a black & white checkered blazer.

Mother and Dad coming out of New York restaurant in about 1941.

The Eberle Named Ray

Circa 1941 - Glenn and the band in a live broadcast for WOR Radio. Dad is seated at the far left with Marion.

Circa 1939 - Dad and Marion Hutton singing a live broadcast for CBS Radio.

Circa 1958 - Ray clapping to the beat of his band.

Circa 1950 - Ray and his Serenade In Blue Orchestra

The Eberle Named Ray

Circa 1939 - Glenn and Dad live broadcast for CBS.

ca 1941 - Ray and The Mods - a music moment.

Circa 1973 - Ray and Tex on CBC television

Circa 1962 - My father with Tex Beneke's Orchestra for a reunion show.

Circa 1976 - Dad with Ray McKinley, drummer with the original Glenn Miller Orchestra.

Circa 1960 - Marion Hutton and Dad rehearsing for reunion album recording.

Late 1950's - front: Dad, Paula Kelly, Tex Beneke and The Modernaires. *Publicity shot courtesy UTM Artists, Ltd.*

Circa 1978 - Tex, Dad, Paula Kelly, Jr., and The Modernaires. Final publicity photos taken of Ray.

The Eberle Named Ray

Dad poolside - early 1940's in southern California.

1967 - St. Thomas on cruise ship, Princessa Leopoldina. Dad,me and Laurie.

May 1967 - Dad in Lake Park doing what he really loved...fishing!

1994 - At my farm with Laurie, me, J.R. and John.

Spring 1968, Riviera Beach, FL - Ray, Jr.'s baptism. (l-r): Dad, Joanne holding J.R., Joanne's father, George (standing in for godfather, Perry Como), and J.R.'s godmother, Jackie Brown. Me and Laurie in front.

The Eberle Named Ray

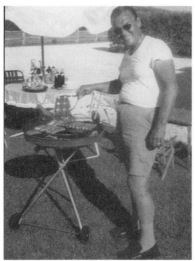

My father, 1965, in charge of cooking, summer in New Jersey.

Me and Laurie with Ray, Jr. in June 1968.

Me and Dad at my 5th birthday party in New Jersey.

1994 - Christmas on my farm with Ray, Jr. (J.R.).

1964 - Me and Dad taking a dip.

The Eberle Named Ray

1967 Joanne and Ray aboard the cruise ship Princessa Leopoldina.

1994 - Christmas with Laurie, Joanne and me.

Chapter Seven

Autumn in northern New Jersey was usually pretty spectacular and my father loved autumn. We looked forward to fiery, red maples and the yellows and oranges set off against smoky gray skies. There is a kind of relentless peace that comes with watching foliage change, die and gracefully fall to the ground. Some leaves fall easily, yet others still possess brilliant color, fighting mother nature by holding on. And holding on. Those are the tenacious ones. It can also be a depressing time of year; no one enjoys watching life slip away.

By the second half of 1963, Laurie and I were traveling almost constantly with Dad. I was three and a handful for my ten-year-old sister to handle but, somehow, she did. My father was drinking very heavily by then. So much so that we noticed the changes in him.

One trip we took with Dad turned out to be a real disaster. By the time we got to our destination, which I think was San Diego, my father was drunk, very drunk. We somehow reached the hotel and shortly after we arrived in our room, my father laid on the bed and began having seizures. The convulsing caused him to roll off the side of the bed and crack his head on the corner of the hotel nightstand. Laurie and I didn't know what to do. The airline stewardesses, who were staying down the hall from us, located the hotel doctor. Laurie and I were escorted to a room where a nice elderly couple stayed. I think we met them on the plane earlier that day. They fed us milk and cookies and treated us kindly until the coast was clear to go back to our own room. My father's seizure stemmed from the drinking. Seizures, like the one he had, can be caused in alcoholics by liver damage. It amazes me that our bodies are intelligent enough to retaliate against our relentless invasions.

In the fall of 1963, Dad, Tex and the reunion crew were working on another album. Once again, Warner Brothers Records produced an album full of wonderful arrangements and a selection of songs that fell a little bit outside the past choices of Miller tunes. Tex and his Orchestra, however, were still playing in the Miller sound. It worked well for them because that is the sound they all began singing to twenty-five years earlier. Dad recorded his version of a then popular song called "Call Me Irresponsible," and it was well-suited to his smooth delivery. The album, appropriately named *Something New*, also included a vivacious arrangement of the theme from *Exodus* (1960) and again worked the Miller style with some conceptual changes including some ballistic percussion from Joey Preston on "Crazy Rhythm" and Tex's feature on "Little Girl Blue." A young Alan Copeland, who had an association with The Modernaires and a good friend of Dad's, did some fantastic arrangements.

Alan Copeland, arranger, friend and Modernaire, remembers:

> *Class, charm wit, heart ... the perfect leading man to front for the brilliant, slightly conservative Glenn Miller ... bringing the romance (hiding in the carefully constructed arrangements) to life with that youthful sincerity and rich, plaintive baritone. He was a smiling, dark, handsome matador crooning the greatest love songs of an age, always winning over the pawing, snorting bulls running wild in the streets of a world gone mad. Ray Eberle ... the antidote for a generation of lovers striving to mask the reality of a world at war. A balladeer who loved to laugh ... the roughness of the road no match for his mischievous twinkle and hearty lust for life.*

> *We first met on a sparkly day in New York ('49) as he cruised up in front of our (The Mods) hotel in a sleek, black caddy convertible. He put me at ease at once with that effortless charm and drove us all out to the NBC studios in Brooklyn for a Bell Telephone Hour salute to the music of Glenn Miller. These salutes would keep bringing us together throughout the years. The longest engagement was a six month (with Tex and a band that would've made Glenn smile) at the Sahara Hotel in Las Vegas. The Casbah Lounge was packed every night, and there, backstage, Ray loved to kid me about my addiction to tuna sandwiches. One evening, he handed me a CAN of*

tuna between two, protesting pieces of limp, white bread. Laughing over his shoulder as he strode out in front of the band to once again charm the fans and bring back those days when girls were courted and wore corsages. He'd sing several of my charts as well as newer things, like, "Lollipops and Roses," "Call Me Irresponsible" and a swinging version of "Tangerine" with a warm nod to brother, Bob.

"EB" ... a gentleman always gentle on my mind ...

The album cover was shot in Lake Tahoe and showed my father, heavier than he had been several months before. He was bloated from the alcohol. Mother was with him during the time of this recording and it necessitated my father giving her daily morphine injections to help ease her pain. Right after Thanksgiving, Mom slipped into a coma and my father had no choice but to rush her back East.

I have a newspaper clipping from the New York *Journal-American* on December 3, 1963 in which an uninformed writer named Dorothy Kilgallen, the society gossip columnist, wrote a premature obituary about my mother. (She regained consciousness after her coma that month.) Dorothy inaccurately wrote that "smooth crooning Ray Eberle had mourned the death of his pretty, young wife, who had succumbed to cancer." This naturally increased the pain in our family. Mother came out of her coma later that month, but the days passed endlessly for her. She occupied a hospital bed permanently by now, but did manage to be home for Christmas. She tried taking care of her personal business, but as the cancer spread to her brain it robbed her of her sight. The last weeks were unbearable for her and for Dad who was now swimming in sorrow and the bottle.

We all had to prepare ourselves somehow to say "good-bye." My father had to say good-bye to twenty-five years of love, great friendship and the mother of his children, business partner, traveling companion, and soul mate. He never was able to say good-bye.

Mother's death crushed him and, as when Glenn died, he reeled, but this was breaking him and causing a void that never healed. On February 18th, 1964, Mother died; my father was never the same and a sadness was in his eyes for the rest of his life.

My father had came home very late from the hospital after taking care of the final business regarding Mother. He fell asleep in the wee hours and arose later that day. My sister, Laurie, had been told about Mom by my sister, Raye. Dad came downstairs to the kitchen and looked at Laurie and spoke quietly.

"She's a brick." No one replied.

My father never said a word to me about my mother's death. In fact, it was understood by the older sisters, uncles, aunts and grandmother that it was not to be mentioned in front of me. I can say that I appreciate the gesture, but she was my mother. Laurie was against not telling me and knew I would get suspicious eventually.

She waited. The day finally came when I asked her. I knew something was fishy because people were always walking around looking like they had been crying, insisting they all had colds. Something just told me that Mother was not in the hospital any longer.

"Where's Mom?" I finally asked my sister, who was relieved that I had asked.

"She went to heaven," she replied.

"Oh." That was all I said, understanding it only on the simplest of levels. I just never saw her again. And her things were gone, too. The pictures of her, her hairbrush, her lipstick, her jewelry box, all things she kept on her dresser. They were all gone.

Then, one day early in March, a woman accompanied Dad to my grandmother's house in Toms River, where I had been staying since shortly after my mother's death. He introduced her to me as "Joanne." I remember looking up at her as she bent down to say, "hello." I could smell her perfume. I eyed her fancy clothes and looked at her face and saw her make-up. Joanne was glamorous like a movie star. I wondered who she was, but felt uneasy the first time we met. I am not sure why. I knew my sister had never seen anyone that made up and beautiful before, either. The big question for us was, *why was she there?*

My father kept his commitments, working was his way of staying out of the raw reality of his life. He had a tour that was beginning in the Midwest. Before he left, my family caught wind of the fact that Joanne was there. Laurie and I still weren't sure why she was there. My two eldest sisters and grandmother knew, however. I remember a lot of tension and crying and weird things said, all that surrounded Joanne's presence. The atmosphere was so bad that my father sent her away for awhile.

Dad had met Joanne in Lake Tahoe the previous November at one of the nightclubs. She was at the time a dancer with a company that was playing at Harrah's at the same time Dad was singing there. They had spent hours talking, one thing led to another and they ended up spending the rest of the night together.

After Mother died, and despite his grief, my father needed to provide someone to take care of his children and his business affairs.

Dad married Joanne the following May: in time, love grew. Three weeks later, he left for the Midwest.

As the summer of 1964 came, Dad, Tex, Paula and The Modernaires were preparing for a long-awaited European tour. It had been in the works for over a year. The band had to be tight, the arrangements sharp, and the singers fresh and bright. My father was neither fresh nor bright then. The singers made their way through the Midwest as a sort of dry run for their trip overseas. They had a new album on Capital Records titled *New Top Hits in the Glenn Miller Style*. And it was as well-received as the previous reunion albums. On this album my father performed a tune, "Stay with Me," that was the theme song from the movie *The Cardinal* (1963). Arranged in the Miller style, the tune was originally a church hymn. I have heard my father perform many different tunes, live and recorded, popular and obscure, but never have I heard him sing with as much passion as on this song. The lyrics, heartfelt and deep, coupled with Dad's strong, smooth baritone voice gave it extraordinary presence.

While on his tour of the Midwest, my father had another seizure. This one was apparently a bad one. Paula was instructed to call Joanne if anything like that happened. Paula and the others were very worried about Dad. Even though he was still able to carry himself through the shows, there was little of him left for anything else. They called Dr. Kline, who was aware of Dad's alcoholism and seizures. Joanne went to the hotel where Dad was staying and, after his show, she met him at his room. While they talked, he had yet another seizure. It was from the alcohol and his liver had sustained some damage. Joanne consulted with Dr. Kline and my father was immediately put on a liquid vitamin mixture called Theron. Theron was geared toward helping stop liver degeneration while hoping for a little regeneration. He drank it religiously. However, he was also told, in no uncertain terms, that he would have to lay off the booze. I can imagine how hard he must have tried to keep it together after years of anesthetizing himself so he could survive from day to day.

Dad returned to Short Hills after his lengthy tour of the Midwest and immediately began preparing for his tour to Europe. He couldn't deal with it. The house was full of memories and there were substantial hospital bills to pay. It was a situation Dad found untenable and he immediately ordered the house be sold. And so Joanne was assigned power of attorney, Dad left for Europe, and our home in Short Hills was up for sale. Joanne was left with a handful, including the miserable task of selling our house and, when not in Toms River with our grandmother, taking care of two children she barely knew.

My father traveled the Scandinavian countries and continued into East Germany. The reunion singers were greeted with great enthusiasm and their tour was proving to be a great success.

Meanwhile, back in the United States, Joanne sold our house and found an apartment in Morristown, New Jersey. By the time my father returned home, we were completely moved into our new surroundings and attempting to adjust to all the changes in our lives.

Chapter Eight

Glenn Miller would have been proud of the Glenn Miller Singers and their success in helping to revive and sustain an era that was bound to slip into history. He would have approved of the way Tex led his own band and of the way my father's voice had matured into the smooth baritone it had become. And once again Ray Eberle lent his voice to the tunes he had made popular for Glenn. Glenn would have had great admiration for Paula and The Modernaires and the polished sound they achieved in every performance. After all, he had handpicked each and every one of his singers. He knew what looked good and sounded good. And, apparently, he knew what would last.

Ray, Tex, Paula and The Modernaires had been riding pretty high for almost a decade. They had enjoyed hundreds of performances together, several new albums and new fans joining the old to cheer them on. My father, in addition, had done some radio and television out of New York City and was looking to do more while managing to maintain his Serenade In Blue Orchestra. Glenn lived on in them.

As for my Dad's personal life, it continued coming apart and his train was grinding to a complete halt as it wobbled up to the platform. He was ill and was about to face the long and final miserable leg of his ride—and he was unable to cope with its turns.

He was not happy to return from Europe to a small, sanitized apartment. He hated apartment living. I am not sure what he expected, but I suspect he was not prepared for the sudden jolt of not being in the home he really loved. This was not a place of memories; he was not in the house where he used to order beer by the case that he stacked on the back porch. He was not in the house where he would get up in the morning, drink a warm beer, vomit and repeat it until it would stay down. Unfortunately, the change was also no change: Daddy was killing himself and there wasn't anything any of us could do, except watch. We loved him and hated to see how much pain he was in.

Ray Eberle was a gentleman with class. I had seen him walk on stage many times and knew he always felt the butterflies. Now, at this stage of his life, I am not sure how he focused; he must have put himself on autopilot. He was gaining weight from consuming large quantities of alcohol and his color was a little off. This was apparent on the last reunion album the Glenn Miller Singers made with Tex Beneke. It was their Christmas album of 1965 and was recorded while my father had the flu. His performance on that album fell a little short of what he was capable even taking into account the flu. His rendition of "White Christmas" was mediocre at best and the first signs that alcoholism was taking its toll were evident. We all watched helplessly.

At around this time, Dad moved us quickly out of apartment living and bought a nice little house in Chatham, New Jersey. It was not Short Hills, but it had a great hill out front for sleigh riding when it snowed. We liked the neighborhood. Laurie and I had to walk quite a few blocks to school, but I was with my sister so I didn't really mind. Things at home with Joanne were still an adjustment. Dad had asked us if we felt comfortable calling her, "Mom," but it took me a while before I felt comfortable doing that.

Laurie and I were still traveling with Dad, and during the school session we simply took schoolwork with us to keep up with the class. One night, while at home, something scary happened. I didn't hear it, but my sister heard it and we later learned that my father had been experiencing a condition called "Delirium Tremens," or commonly, "D.T.'s." When an alcoholic is suddenly deprived of alcohol, this condition can develop for short periods and can scare the heck out of anyone who sees or hears it. Commonly, an addict will start seeing and experiencing things that aren't there. My father was in his room, banging his arm against the wall trying to rid himself of the imaginary things that were crawling on him.

The following year, we went to Florida where Dad picked up some work. It also served as a vacation. My father loved fishing, but was not all that crazy about heat. We all felt a little depressed upon our returning to Chatham only to find that we'd been snowed out and we had to dig our way into our house. After doing that a couple of times that year, Dad moved us to Florida. At the time, my sister and I liked the idea, but in retrospect, I am not really sure how good an idea it turned out to be either for all of us or professionally—for my father. Once again, we packed and moved. The frequent uprooting was becoming unsettling and it felt more and more like we were running.

After moving to Florida in 1966, Laurie and I were registered in school and Dad worked on keeping his career on track. Initially, he picked up work at the Red Lion in Jupiter and places like The Fountain Bleu, in Miami. Gradually, he began getting more and more work as people in the largest retirement state discovered Ray Eberle had set down new roots.

Joanne had a lot of adjusting to do as well. Not necessarily from the move to Florida, but more so for the change in her career status. Joanne Genthen was no stranger to show business; she had spent many years of sacrifice working toward her own accomplishments. She had begun her career as a ballet dancer and, as time went on, diversified into working with traveling dance companies. Joanne appeared as a dancer in the 1955 movie, *Oklahoma* and had an appearance in the 1958, Alfred Hitchcock thriller, *Vertigo* playing the mythological Carlotta Valdez.

She continued to travel and dance and, in 1959, appeared as the witch in a movie starring Sean Connery, called *Darby O'Gill and the Little People*. Her career, up to that point, had been satisfying and productive. My father believed that Joanne would not be able to handle his career and children properly if she continued her own career in the business, so he asked her to retire her career. He believed one person in a household in show business was enough because it was not predictable and can take away the stability needed for children and home.

Joanne walked away from her own hard-earned career for a chance to make a life with my father, disastrous as the situation was. She didn't know too much about children and knew even less about life with a sick man she didn't know very well. It must have been hell.

Dad obtained a contract to perform in the cruise ship circuit, which had become a growing attraction for entertainers. In 1967 and 1968, the four of us traveled to San Juan, St.

Thomas, Nassau and other islands in the Atlantic and Caribbean. The cruise ships employed a Portuguese crew and it was quite comical trying to communicate on the most basic level with them. Once during breakfast, my father asked for catsup for his scrambled eggs and the waiter returned with maple syrup.

Traveling on the cruise ship offered us the opportunity to really let go. It was exciting, and we felt free to take a much needed exhale. The past few years had been difficult. The household was more strict and there was unfamiliar tension as Dad struggled day by day to balance his career and disease. All of the changes were near devastating to the family. The cruises served as an oasis from the tumultuous life we led. My father seemed to enjoy them very much and, even though he rehearsed most afternoons and did a couple of shows a night, he managed to enjoy smelling the salt air and basking in the warm sun. It was therapeutic.

For me, I finally was able to feel like a kid at play. On one cruise I jumped into the ship's salt water pool during rough seas. I had never experienced a pool so turbulent and panicked a little after I realized I couldn't get back to the edge. Paul Anka thoughtfully jumped in and calmly guided me back. Laurie and I became friends with Betty Clooney's girls and we played together throughout the cruise. I was a "kid at play" for the first time in a long time.

Dad began a period in which he was late for a few jobs and missed a couple all together. He'd say he had a sore throat or some other excuse. We knew that this kind of historically atypical behavior stemmed from his drinking, and it made it harder and harder for him to find work. It became a chore keeping his schedule full enough to support us. We had been in Florida two years and already had moved several times, growing increasingly familiar with a feast or famine existence. My father didn't handle money very well and he didn't have a handle on himself. We moved repeatedly. House. Apartment. House. Apartment. Whatever financial means necessitated at that particular time.

Life was hard enough for Dad's career being so far away from an entertainment Mecca like New York City. It was further complicated by the disease of alcoholism. In addition to this, the times and tastes were once more in flux. The 1960's had their own special style that worked against my father's style and his ability to get work. He was down to booking hotel lounges around the state of Florida.

Our lives also continued with changes. Joanne brought her ill father to live with us and apartment living was hard for five people. In addition, Joanne became pregnant. Toward the end of her pregnancy, when traveling was out of the question for her, Laurie and I went back to traveling with Dad and taking with us our schoolwork. This at least made it easier for those remaining at home.

In March of 1968, Dad got a call at the motel in St. Petersburg that Joanne was in labor. Laurie was fourteen, I was eight and Dad left us at the motel that day and flew back to West Palm Beach. Dad had an engagement scheduled that evening back in St. Petersburg. We didn't hear from him all day and when he arrived back in St. Pete, he was drunk. With only a couple of hours before his show, he strolled into the room and told us about the new baby. It was a boy and they'd named him Ray. Laurie and I were thrilled, but we were also afraid for Dad because we weren't sure whether he was going to be able to do his show that night without falling down. Amazingly once again, the autopilot kicked in and we were relieved when he came back after the show, still standing.

I know Dad was excited about having a baby boy in his life after raising four girls. Ray was a good father. Better than most, especially where intentions were concerned. He wasn't the most emotional man, but he knew how to treat his children. I spent many nights from the time my mother was ill until then asking Dad to come into my room at night to rub my head when I couldn't sleep. It was a comforting thing. He'd sit on the edge of my bed, lean in, and he would rub my head softly and methodically until I fell asleep. I hoped my father would stay well enough to offer the same to young Ray.

Chapter Nine

Ray Junior, or J.R. as he was playfully known, had my father's features, deep brown eyes, dark hair and olive complexion. He was, indeed, a bouncing baby boy and keeping him down was a chore. My father was nearly fifty years old when J.R. was born. He had already raised a generation of children and was now moving into another. Joanne, on the other hand, had never really been exposed to babies and had a bit of a time adjusting.

Dad finally gave in to the fact that Joanne needed to go back to some part of her career; the thought was that modeling fit the bill and in turn would help pay the bills. Her plan was to begin doing some runway modeling which meant she would need to lose the weight gained for childbirth. Joanne was tall and, at the age of thirty-four, was used to being slender. The fact that she had to lose weight at all upset her a great deal. Nevertheless by the fall season, she was ready to begin.

Dad was working when he could, flying to Chicago and New York wherever opportunity presented itself, but by the second half of the 1960's it was very difficult to maintain a full career. He was still willing to sing the songs he'd been singing since he was eighteen, but the work just was not there. Compounding this was his occasional tardiness and missed dates: that hurt his reputation as being reliable.

Tex and his band ran into some of the same difficulties. He told me that many of the old ballrooms were being turned into, of all things, bowling alleys. Nostalgia was becoming a hard sell. Paula Kelly and The Modernaires likely experienced the same issues. The only thing one could do was to call upon those who had employed them in the past. New opportunities were scarce.

Meanwhile, Joanne was enjoying her newfound venture into modeling as the lead runway model for Jordan Marsh. She was feeling comfortable and confident on the runway and it gave her the opportunity to take a break from the realities of motherhood. By the spring of 1969, she began feeling ill, in an all too familiar way. Indeed, she was pregnant again. Joanne had just begun enjoying rejuvenating her career and going through another pregnancy didn't seem thrilling. The children would be eighteen months apart in age. Two babies in diapers would be more than a challenge.

In October of 1969, Joanne gave birth to her second child, John Robert. At that time, Dad was still partaking greedily in the grog and was not very productive around the house. He didn't change diapers, assist with feedings, help with laundry or help with their meals. It was like having three children in the house. Those first several days drove Joanne to the brink of insanity and just days after John was born she ended up back in the hospital, this time for exhaustion and depression. She took the much needed rest and eased back into the duties at hand. Joanne also contemplated a return to modeling, quicker this time because she had less weight to lose.

Life continued. The approach of Christmas brought an added urgency to the everyday chores, as she prepared a nice Christmas for the boys. I had moved back to New Jersey to live with my maternal grandmother, Nana, earlier that year, so there was no additional help to look after the boys at home. Joanne tried decorating a Christmas tree, buying gifts, planning a holiday meal and keeping up with her regular agenda.

Finally, one day, she just sat on the floor in tears, fed up with everything, and everyone, especially the fear that my father would never stop drinking. Dad was hiding six packs in the bathroom trash cans, believing she would never find them. On Christmas morning, she stood holding J.R. by the hand and John in her arms. She told my father that she couldn't live that way any longer. And, at that point, she contemplated taking her boys and leaving for good. Things were bottoming out.

One day, shortly after New Year's Day in 1970, my father stopped drinking. To my knowledge Dad never touched another drop of alcohol after that day. Becoming sober doesn't take willpower, rather willingness to surrender it to God, day by day, not lifetime by lifetime. My father shared with me his experience of the night before he chose sobriety. As he laid in bed, a very bright light appeared to him giving him an unexplainable sense of peace and comfort. He said he asked God for help, and it came. Dad told me that sobriety came as naturally as breathing and from that day on, he never again let his faith in God waiver. He was emerging from a cloud he had hidden behind for years and was willing to face what he'd been running from.

Tom Sheils, manager and agent, reflects on this time.

I met your Dad in December of 1938 at the Glen Island. I booked the band on their day off (they worked six days a week) to play a high school dance. Glenn's band, along with Ray, played all summer on and off and Ray and I became pretty close friends then.

I imagine your Dad's alcoholism did hurt his voice a little, but more so his reputation. And, I do know that after he became a reformed alcoholic, he craved a lot of ice cream for some reason. Joanne said he would go through a quart a day, if she let him. The older he got, though, the better his voice got! I'm sure it was tough for Ray as well as the family, to go through that period in his life, but he licked it! He licked it and came back stronger and better than ever! Your father was a dear friend that I adored very much and I miss him.

Ray was beginning to get to know his sons the way he had known his girls when they were little. He was enjoying that part of his newfound sobriety. He was also beginning to enjoy performing again. For the first months of 1970 and the first few years after that, my father concentrated on regaining as much health as he could, but equally as important, regaining his reputation in the business. That meant a lot to him and he'd worked to maintain it.

One of the greatest things that happened to him while he was recovering was the full return of his beautiful voice. In fact, he not only regained what he had temporarily lost, but many people, including myself, thought he sounded better than he ever had in his whole career. It was as though his voice came back with an added gift. The creaminess and clarity of his baritone was purer than ever. There was something else, though. His voice had become a voice that could once again express emotion.

Dad's voice was returning and he was willing to show others how responsible and dependable he could be for the business, but there just wasn't much work to be found. He did an occasional date with Tex and The Modernaires, but they were far fewer than they had been a few short years before. The same was true for his Serenade In Blue Orchestra. There simply was not enough work. Finally, for the first time in his life, he felt he needed to work some other type of job to make ends meet. He thought carefully and accepted a part time offer as a salesman on a used car lot. That seemed a little far removed for someone who was used to wearing a tuxedo, singing all evening and signing autographs at the end of the night. The problem was that my father was a little too honest. I am not implying that car salesmen are liars. I do, however, believe there is a difference between being honest and being too honest.

He told me once that clients approached him looking for a car and they were interested in one particular sedan. He listened to them for a while. "Look, I know you really like that car, but believe me, you don't really want that car. It doesn't run very well. If you want an automobile that is the best deal for the money, I'll take you over here and show you this one, but you definitely don't want that car."

He stayed with selling cars for a while. Then, work began picking up slowly again. People were once more seeking out Ray Eberle. They trusted him, supported his newfound sobriety and rallied behind him and his enthusiasm to keep bringing back the music he knew best how to sing. Ray looked healthy and his voice was back, better than ever!

Helen Robertson, family friend:

I met your father and Joanne in, probably, 1970 for a baby-sitting job. Well, I can remember Ray always sitting in his big, oversized leather chair ... with large arms on it and a matching foot stool. He never put his shoes next to the chair or anywhere else on the floor ... they were always set on a little ledge underneath the table next to his leather chair.

And, whenever the boys wanted their shoes put on, they would automatically go to him. Ray would sit them up on the huge arm of his chair and it's not as though they were too young to know how to put their shoes on, but they just liked it when your father did it. And, so he did. But, oh, did he love all his children ...

During those five years prior to Dad's sobriety, Joanne, our "new Mom," really stuck with us. Many days were dismal as she worried about my father. Taking care of us kids was no picnic, either. I was sick quite often with upset stomachs and Laurie seemed to corner the market on "pink eye."

I remember one bad scene in Texas before the boys were born in which Joanne threatened to walk out. Joanne had canceled the outing she and Dad planned because he had gotten himself too drunk. The baby sitter was canceled and Laurie and I were called into their room. Dad said that he was a bum and that Joanne was leaving and that it was his fault. My sister and I didn't say much, but I remember Joanne bent down to us and reassured us that she was not going to leave us because she loved us. She stuck with us when many would have been long gone. I loved her for that and was eternally grateful for her unselfish acts.

Finally, after many lean, hard years for big band music, things began to look up for Dad, thanks in part to Walt Disney. In the mid-1970's, Orlando, Florida became the second location in America to house a Disney Theme Park. And soon Disney World became just as popular, if not more so, as its original counterpart, Disneyland. Almost immediately, Dad got offers to sing in one of the most popular resort hotels on Disney's grounds. The Contemporary Hotel housed the Top of the World lounge/theater in the uppermost part of the hotel. It was a place offering adults the kind of quality entertainment to which people spending the money were entitled. My father was enjoying himself more at this point in his career than he ever had—and, his voice was in absolute prime condition. Also, he was more relaxed on stage taking more time to talk between songs, often relating a funny story about himself.

My father had become a humble man. He could laugh at himself and that only increased the natural charisma he possessed. Still a young man in his mid fifties, Ray looked good and sounded good.

The Contemporary Hotel liked my father so much they extended his run for weeks at a time. Now in my teens I really liked to visit him in what was the presidential suite. It had four rooms to romp in with my best friend Linda in addition to lots of cool room service and free theme park tickets!

Dad's repertoire, at that point, reflected a variety of songs which collectively expressed who he had become as a singer. He was less afraid to step outside the lines and blended a nice song list of old and new, ballad and up tempos, popular and obscure. Many nights, he began his show with a medium Swing version of a song titled, "Where or When," leading into a repertoire that obviously would include "Serenade In Blue" and "At Last," which he was still happy to sing.

Watching him on one of the first nights, dolled up for the evening, I remember how handsome he looked in his tuxedo and I could smell his cologne. Dad had a smell that, coupled with his cologne, was unique to him. It was Daddy. It was the same smell I remembered those nights he rubbed my head until I fell asleep. He looked over at me, and smiled a broad smile; "Finally," I thought, "the son of a gun is having the time of his life."

Arlene and John Benko, family friends:

> *I remember most of the time, when we would pull up in front of the house, your father would be on that riding lawn mower of his, wearing Bermuda shorts and an old fishing hat. He was such a nice man ... always friendly and so handsome.*

> *John and I had only seen your father at home in a casual situation until one time, he and Joanne asked us to go with them to Disney World in Orlando because your father was singing at the Top of the World in the Contemporary Hotel. I had never seen Ray perform before. Joanne and I were all dressed up*

and I can remember Ray being introduced. He walked out clean, wearing a tuxedo and looking more handsome than ever! And then he started to sing. My God, it was like a transformation! That voice just melted me and Ray had so much charisma. He loved being up there and the people loved seeing him there, too. I'll never forget that. It was like night and day, because at home, he was just a "regular Joe."

One day, my father got a call from an old acquaintance of his who was pitching a new idea for a tour that was pretty extensive. Les Brown had made his own mark in music history long ago, and he was now proposing a fresh, new concept that caught my father's interest. Les asked my father if he was interested in becoming a part of his new show. Not just as a vocalist, but as the star of his own section of the show, billing a sort of yesteryear package. Dad went for it and they were a huge success.

Les was a great bandleader who ran a fairly tight outfit. He had enormous success and longevity in the business while remaining all along a very sweet man. Much of his early success was due in part to singer, Doris Day, who with Les had a great hit with "Sentimental Journey." It was their signature song, so to speak. After she departed for motion pictures, he kept growing in popularity because of his clean, agreeable style. He, too, was unique. Once again, Dad had the freedom to be himself and express his artistry the best way he knew how.

In 1976, we were still living north of West Palm Beach. I had returned the year before to live with Dad because I'd missed him so much. We talked a lot the first few weeks I returned. He was glad I was home, too. We were having this crazy conversation about his getting older and how that idea made him look at things in a different way. I thought, he's not old! What is he talking about? Then, he turned to me suddenly and his expression softened. He looked at me for a few moments.

"You remind me so much of your mother." Then, he smiled.

He had never said anything like that to me before. He could never even talk about my mother. I knew how much pain it brought him to do so. That one moment spoke volumes and I had waited for a long time to hear something from him about her. It was perfect.

That same year, 1976, my father again became part of music history. For the very first time, Dad and Uncle Bob performed together, on the same stage. Most would have thought that two brothers who were in the same business, singing the same era of music, who were both popular, would've performed together. It hadn't happened until this day.

It was actually Uncle Bob's engagement. He, too, was appearing at the Top of the World, with his longtime singing partner, Helen O'Connell. They were good together and had spent decades sharing the same stage. Helen was such a sweet lady and very funny, too. That's one of the reasons she and Uncle Bob worked so well together. One day, Helen was notified that she had been nominated for an Emmy Award for her work as host of the Miss America and Miss Universe pageants. While the honor of receiving an Emmy nomination was wonderful, it left a void in the show with Bob. He did what good brothers should do. He called up his brother.

A hand-held cassette tape of this performance is all that exists, but it documents a performance that is funny, relaxed, and in very good voice. After my uncle belted out "Sentimental Journey," "Birth of the Blues," and "The Breeze and I," he introduced Dad with obvious pride and real admiration. He wanted people to know that their relationship had not gone the way others had. They had always been close and didn't possess any animosity or sibling rivalry. My father and uncle had always just been Ray and Bob, the brothers.

Dad sang a chilling version of "What Are You Doing the Rest Of Your Life" and followed that up with a wonderful, Swing arrangement of "Pennies From Heaven." The repartee went back and forth through the performance.

"Wow, that was a long note you held ... and it was on key, too. You'd better knock the stuff off," Uncle Bob teased.

"You know, Bob, I've got a real goodie coming up here. I've gotten a lot of mileage out of this one. It's great. You know, you and Helen could've done well with this one. It's a real beauty." Then, Dad

broke into a Swing version of "Tangerine." Uncle Bob just laughed.

They ended with a medley of some of their favorite tunes, sung mostly in duet. They seemed relaxed and truly to have enjoyed the rarity of the experience.

I witnessed the changes my father went through since 1964 and it had been a rough road. My father had survived adversity many times in his life and made it through as he would this time, too.

Two brothers cutting up. Uncle Bob and my father around 1940 taking a break from work.

Chapter Ten

It seemed inconceivable to me that my father had suffered a heart attack. It was pretty hard for most of us to believe.

The summer of 1979 appeared endless. Dad hadn't been sick for very long and his illness seemed very sudden. He had seemed fine, but during a visit from my sister, Laurie, he complained about the pain in his arm and chest. Joanne took him to the hospital to have him checked out. The doctors and nurses did every kind of prodding and probing test they knew how to do. My father was in intensive care and being monitored very closely. He wasn't used to being poked at by doctors. He rarely ever even got a cold. Intravenous lines, medication, catheters, all of that didn't sit well with him.

As he lay in the hospital bed, I think he was in deep denial. He was scared. Dad felt his mortality tugging and taunting him. While Laurie and Joanne were visiting him in intensive care one day, he broke down and cried. He simply said he couldn't believe he'd had a heart attack.

My father felt out of control, totally. He had to get used to the idea that he was not in control. After a few days, he was released, but returned for more tests, including the dreaded treadmill test.

Now, Dad may have been handsome and strong, but he was not physically fit. He had never kept any regular exercise program; his idea of getting out and working out was taking a ride on his riding lawn mower.

After his treadmill test, doctors determined the best way to handle the blockages and damage done to his heart was to perform a triple bypass surgery. My father agreed, but his doctors recommended he wait for the surgery as scar tissue was supposed to form around his damaged heart before it was safe to perform the bypass. So, with medication in hand, Dad headed home to wait out his time and to try and rest. I think my father thought he was going to pick up his engagements where he had left them prior to his hospitalization. He even talked about his next date as if he was actually going to make it. Denial can be cruel.

I received a phone call from my father after his release from the hospital. He called to explain the surgery, what it entailed and approximately when he was scheduled for the whole ordeal. He sounded a little tired to me on the phone that night, but I was just glad to hear his voice.

"Hi'ya, kiddo! How's it going?"

"Hi, Dad! How are you? Did you break out of the hospital?"

"They actually let me out, can you believe it? I must have been a real pain in the butt! Listen, I want to talk to you about something. The doctors know what's wrong with me and they've asked me to consider triple bypass surgery."

"God, Dad! Can't they put you on a diet or give you medicine or something?" I was shocked by his news.

"No, honey, this would really be the best thing. Besides, when I'm done, I'll be better than new. Hey, I'm gonna breeze right through this thing. Don't worry about it. It'll be all over before you know it." I was at a loss for words.

"So, ... you're all right with this then?"

"Yeah. They do this kind of surgery all the time and I'm not worried. Just tired. I'll let you know when they are going to do this thing, O.K.?"

"O.K., Daddy. Hey Dad? I love you."

"I love you, too, kiddo."

I had a pretty strange feeling that night. I understood what Dad explained to me, but I suppose I was wearing my own coat of denial.

It was hot that following Saturday morning in August, as New Jersey summers tend to be. Dennis (Gordon), my fiancé at the time, and I were making breakfast at about ten o'clock when the phone rang. I ran over and answered it. I heard the voice on the other end say, "hello." I answered back, thinking I was talking to Laurie who lived nearby. After a pause, she asked for Dennis. It wasn't unusual for them to talk because Dennis and Laurie had become like brother and sister.

I handed the phone to him. He stared at me blankly and began to speak. He listened for what seemed long periods of time. His voice was quiet and he didn't say much. I stood at my stove, stirring scrambled eggs when the thought occurred to me that Dennis was not talking to my sister.

Oh my God, I thought. I realized it was Joanne and I knew instantaneously that something was very wrong. I refused to believe what I was thinking, which was that this was "the call." The call to say my father was dead. Nah, I thought. I just talked to him. He seemed fine! I turned around slowly and caught a glimpse of Dennis' expression. He looked wan. I knew, oh God ... I knew.

I turned back to face the stove and shut off the eggs. He hung up the phone softly and didn't say anything to me. If I spoke first, he wouldn't have a chance to talk. If he didn't talk, he couldn't say anything bad. Therefore, it would all right.

"Breakfast is definitely ready, ummm, smells good, doesn't it?" I raised my eyes to meet his, but only for an instant. It took everything he had to crack the faint smile I received. I knew.

As we sat and forced ourselves to eat, it was very hard to make casual conversation. All of a sudden, my shock wore off. I rinsed the dishes at the sink. Dennis came up behind me and didn't speak. I stopped, leaned over toward the freezer and proceeded to rip the freezer door off the hinges with one yank. Dennis, literally, had to hold me in place to prevent me from going berserk. After several moments of unabashed hysterics I finally pulled away and spoke.

"Why? HOW?! I don't understand how? I just talked to him on the phone. He was all right. What happened? What the hell happened?"

Dennis went on to tell me about his phone conversation with Joanne earlier.

That morning, a short time before Joanne's call, my father had died at home. It was August 25th, 1979. He was only sixty. Dad and I told each other we loved each other two days earlier. My heart ached, I missed him instantly.

Dad had gotten up very early that morning and had been coughing, apparently from a cold he'd picked up at the hospital. Because the medicine he was taking tended to relax him so much, it was hard for him to control his cough. He wasn't looking well, so Joanne woke the boys and sent them still in their pajamas to a neighbor's house. Evidently, John, who was only nine then, walked by Dad's bedroom and saw him slumped over on the bed, so he knew something was wrong. After my father's collapse, the medics were called, but it was too late. His relentless coughing apparently triggered another heart attack.

At the time I found out about my father's passing, Laurie was still unaware of it. Joanne tried calling Laurie, but when she was unable to reach her. I was going to be the bearer of the worst possible news she could hear. Joanne felt I'd be better equipped to tell her considering she had a hard time telling me.

Dennis and I arrived at Laurie's a short time later only to find she hadn't returned yet. I left a note on Laurie's door and tried not to sound too alarming. Dennis and I went home to wait for her call. She never called. Instead, she drove right over and flew up the stairs to my apartment. When she reached the top, she had a look of horror on her face.

"What's wrong? Did Dad have to go into emergency surgery?" I stood and looked at her briefly. At that moment, she looked lost like a little girl. Now it was my turn to tell her about the loss of a parent.

"Laurie, he's gone." It was all I could think of to say.

Laurie's legs buckled, but I scooped her up before she hit the ground. She was tiny, like my mother, and I easily carried her ninety pounds onto my bed. Michael (DiPilla), my nephew, had been told and we all sort of hung together and cried, and made plans. Dennis bought the three of us airline tickets for the next morning for Atlanta, Georgia, the final place my father called home. There, we would have to say our final good-bye to our father.

I never expected him to leave, at least not that early. And, I never thought about his dying. He was my Daddy, with the chest and heart of a lion and I missed being able to smell his cologne again.

Friends and family were in charge of shuttling incoming family members from the airport to my father's house. None of us knew what to expect when it came to the press or how to navigate these waters of grief: a thick, dark pool of sorrow, anger and incredulity. Seldom had I swam those waters.

Chapter Eleven

Laurie, Michael and I arrived at Hartsfield Airport the following evening. We were greeted at the airport by friends, who were gracious enough to escort us to Dad's Douglasville home. I remember that it was the first time Michael had ever flown and he'd had such a great time that day, pretending to fly the plane. His eyes became enormous as the earth quickly shrank beneath us. Michael's enjoyment helped make the trip bearable. To Michael, it simply was an adventure. To my sister and I, it was uncertainty and dread.

As we left the airport for Dad's house, there was little said among us. Pulling into the driveway I saw the familiar cars parked in the garage.

Oh, look! There's Dad's car, I thought.

I felt an awful combination of excitement and horror. The smells and sights and feelings were all the same as they had always been, but there was a darkness of grief that wasn't there before. The loss began to press in and my denial, that had kept me afloat, was giving way to the reality.

I thought about Joanne and what she must be feeling after losing a husband. I did not look forward to opening that door. Inside the kitchen I heard the television on in the nearby family room. How incredible it was that I could smell him, the food he ate, the clothes he wore, his cologne, his pipe tobacco. It all lingered. I was not scared of what I would find but, rather, of what I knew was gone.

Joanne was in the family room sitting on the floor, staring at the television until she looked up and saw us standing there. We didn't say anything for a long time, but only embraced and cried. I could see that she was in shock. We talked about what family was next scheduled to arrive.

Uncle Bob was on his way and my sister, Raye Ellen, was also en route. There were friends that came and went and there was food everywhere. You would have thought we were about to embark on a goodwill trip to a third world country. The generosity was everywhere. People brought or made food, they cleaned, they taxied to and from the airport and they were there to hug anyone who was in need. Support and love came from people we didn't even know. Lots of them. All those years of performing for fans and crowds of people and they wanted us to know, they too felt a loss. I could only tell them I, too, was sorry for their loss.

As we all sort of got our bearings that night, I eventually saw J.R. and John, too. They didn't really say a lot. They were eleven and nine years old and understood that Dad wasn't coming back, but at that age, the whole picture didn't seem quite in focus. And I understood that because I was myself only nineteen. Their imaginations filled in what they didn't understand.

Joanne seemed pretty out of it and admitted later to having very little memory of the days surrounding Dad's death. While she seemed to be handling the tasks of the funeral arrangements and scheduling newspaper interviews, when it came to the rest, she basically slid through on a wing and a prayer. After all, she had the boys to contend with and watch over. I admired her courage.

Fairburn is a small town not too far from Douglasville, and it was there that we attended an open casket wake. I realized this was the first time I was going to see Dad in a number of months and I was apprehensive. I vividly remember all the flowers that surrounded my father as he rested. One in particular caught my eye because I knew instinctively whom it was from. I noticed a very large wreath sitting on a tripod stand with little scrolls of musical notes that encircled the arrangement. Tex Beneke: it was, indeed, a last sentiment from a man who truly loved my father.

My father looked like he was sleeping. I was glad he hadn't suffered long with an illness that, like my mother's, took her one piece at a time. Viewing him I thought, If he looks so good, why isn't he alive?

J.R. was not coping with this very well because he had seen my father's casket opened hours before while Joanne was checking on the arrangements. It was a shock to him. He wasn't expecting to see his dad anymore at all.

The next day was the funeral and the service. What seemed like hordes of media filled the church and the outlying area. I first saw them outside, setting up cameras at the back door, but I wasn't sure why. When my family and I adjourned to our seats inside the church, I saw cameras set up along the pew perimeters, waiting for the service to begin. What did they want? This was a funeral, for God's sake! For the first time, I remember feeling angry toward the press and I know my judgment had become distorted. I knew people had a right to know these things and that Dad had chosen a life and job that put him very much in the public eye. This was personal though, wasn't it?

At the end of the service as the family followed the casket down the center aisle toward the back door, I realized what all the cameras outside had set up for. They were poised to capture our emotions, the mourning family, as we followed Dad's casket out to the waiting doors of the hearse. I felt disgusted and I'm sure my expression showed it. I know my face didn't look too happy on the news report that night.

Joanne had his remains cremated and shipped to Hoosick Falls, but that didn't seem real, either.

I was nineteen years old. I considered myself fairly mature, but in reality I was just as impressionable as any other young lady my age. As I matured and grew older, my respect for Dad's contributions to music grew and I became more keenly aware of his unique class, charm and style. I was so damn proud of who he was as a father and entertainer and as a recovering alcoholic. Ray spent the last ten years of his life sober and, as for his career, I do believe he was beginning to have the time of his life. I accepted him for who he was, for who he wasn't, and for what he could achieve. I celebrated his "limitless limits."

And that set me free.

Ray Eberle, famous big band singer and father

After being hired by Glenn, I think the reason for my conceit was that Bob really was a good singer and he had been singing for about three years and he had records out and he was doing real good with Jimmy Dorsey. I just thought that because he was my brother that I was going to be a terrific singer right away, too. This is what prompted me to think like I was

*thinking, when we (the band) did the first radio pro-
gram, that every little note I put in there was a gem in
that microphone, that it was all going to come out ter-
rifically, you know? I just didn't believe it was me at
all. I thought they were pulling tricks on me or something else! But, I did, after that, have a whole different opinion of myself. As a matter of fact, I think I
went in the complete opposite direction and became
an introvert and it was to the point that, I remember
one time Glenn said to me, "What are you feeling so
backward about yourself for? These people didn't just
come to see me. They came to see you and listen to
you, too. And, they paid their money. Go on out there
and belt 'em out for them. Don't be afraid of it." He'd
say things like that to me, which encouraged me, so
it just took time.*

*That's the kind of education that there was then
that there is not now for anyone going into the business. There is no school for it. It is just something
you've got to go through and pull your own weight
and get it done or out you go. It's hard knocks, but
that's the way it is. Just experience.*

*And, the main thing is to feel good with the peo-
ple out there because, good Lord, they're with you. It
doesn't seem that way at first. I don't know, it seems
like they're the enemy. I don't know where that feeling ever comes from, but, all of a sudden, it seems
like you get the feeling that they are really with you.*

It was hard to let go of Dad after years of sharing his life.
Those who knew him fewer years might wonder about what
they might have missed. The boys both felt a little cheated,
and rightfully so. They were both young when they had to
give up their father. John revealed to me that he just never
looked at Dad and considered him old. Dad had my oldest sister when he was twenty-one and fathered John nearly thirty
years later. There's nothing wrong with that as long as the risk
is understood.

There are a lot of things I wish I could have shared with Dad, too. I had a successful singing career of my own and wished he could have been there to cheer me on, or even share a verse of "Serenade In Blue" with me. Ray, Jr., told me that if he could change anything about the way he'd raise his son, he simply would try to give more time. He always admired Dad's dedication to his work. My father provided for us and that will never go unappreciated. The family had many memories of Ray, but in 1979, we had one final task. That task was to let him go.

Ray Eberle was sent home to Hoosick Falls, New York, to be near his beloved mother, Margaret and father, Jack. The stone reads, "Eberle" on one side and, "O'Brien" on the other. When I arrived at the cemetery for the first time to visit, I felt an immense sense of peace. I felt grateful for having been a part of this man's life. It was fitting that he ended his journey where it began years before. That thought brought a broad smile to my face and a million memories, memories I thought I had lost, returned.

And then I could smell his cologne.

Late 1970's Ray and Tex Beneke's Orchestra in southern California amphitheater.

The Eberle Named Ray

Afterthoughts

Ray Eberle had a wonderful life full of the magic of music and of family and children and grandchildren and laughs. My father was no Einstein, nor was he Superman. He was as mortal as men can be and as sensitive and loving a father as anyone could ever hope for. He taught his family a lot about living, how to endure and proceed to surpass any obstacles that limit you.

After my father died, I had a fantasy that he had been abducted by foreign spies to become a double agent and that he would escape one day to return to us. Of course, I knew that was not true, but I wanted to invent as many fantasies as I possibly could to keep him alive. I know now, however, that he is alive and well in my memories of us and in my heart. Whenever I pass by a mirror I am reminded of him.

I dream about him from time to time, usually when I am going through a crisis. It's funny, but it seems to be his way of telling me that everything is all right. At least, that's what he tells me in my dreams.

Years after his death, Dad's tenth grandchild was born. His name, too, is Ray Eberle, although he is known to most as Tray. He sees pictures of that handsome man known by many names: Ray, Eb, Jim, the young man in the romance department, Daddy and Poppy. Tray is young right now but he will learn all I have to tell him about his grandfather, the man Tray refers to as "Pee Paw." He will learn all his stories and jokes and all that I have preserved in this book.

I hope I have succeeded in conveying this man's contributions to one of the most important musical eras of our time. Dad's professional and personal lives were testimony to that. I am proud to have known him.

Acknowledgments

I am not the biological mother of any child, but if I were, this book would be it. I awoke many nights at two in the morning to nurture and console this project. Together, we laughed a lot and cried a lot and, at times, got a little lost.

Eight years have passed since I began this journey. It wasn't until I faced my own adversity, in the form of a serious health condition, that I felt emotionally mature enough to see this story through.

My deepest gratitude goes, of course, to those who have unselfishly contributed their time, love and memories. From the bottom of my heart, I would like to thank: Perry Como, Alan Copeland, Johnny Best, Billy May, Tex Beneke, Paula Kelly, Jr., Tom Sheils, Paul Tanner, Bernie Fox, Bert Kosow, Tino Barzey, Helen and Bob Robertson and John and Arlene Benko. My deepest love and thanks to my family, who allowed me passage into their memories … Walt and Olga Eberle, Al Eberle, my sisters, Nancy, Re-ro, and Laurie, my brothers, John and Ray, my stepmother, Joanne. Especially to my mother and Dad, who have sent their love and support from the other side, unseen, but heard.

Index